PRAISE FOR *EMERGING G*

"*Emerging Gospel Movements: The Role of Catalysts* is a welcome contribution to the growing literature on church planting movements with unique attention given to the role of catalysts who facilitate and help advance church multiplication. With numerous case studies and personal stories from around the world, Gene Wilson offers readers a both inspiring and informative resource."

CRAIG OTT, Professor at Trinity Evangelical Divinity School and author of *The Church on Mission* and *Teaching and Learning across Cultures*

"*Emerging Gospel Movements* is a welcomed book in the emerging field of church planting movements during what is considered the facilitator era of missions. Gene Wilson's chapter on gospel movements in the New Testament presents an excellent foundation for understanding movements today. The realistic portrayal of movements in various continents and in a diversity of environments gives inspiration, instruction, and hope. This book will help pastors, missionaries and movement leaders assess and engage wisely with God's amazing movement work."

ROY OKSNEVAD, All People Director, Muslim Ministries, author of *The Gospel for Muslims* and *The Burden of Baggage*

"The role of missionaries in many places is changing from frontline church planting practitioners to coaches and catalysts of deeply committed national leaders and church planters. In *Emerging Gospel Movements*, my friend and colleague, Gene Wilson, gives a thoroughly biblical foundation for what God is doing in these movements. Practical principles and real-life stories will help church planting catalysts maximize their effectiveness in coming alongside these emerging gospel movements around the world. I've watched Gene work and minister around the world, and I highly recommend this book to anyone interested in understanding and engaging these movements for maximum gospel impact."

KEVIN KOMPELIEN, President of the Evangelical Free Church of America

"Movement ministry has already permanently shifted the focus of many in the Great Commission workforce. A good number of these leaders are not Western leaders. They observe the simple yet strategic ways that the gospel moved out in the first few centuries and seek to live that sort of ministry themselves. This emphasis will not be a fad that comes and goes in the church. A book on the topic which is neither critical, nor naïve championing, has fertile soil in the missiological community right now."

TED ESLER, President of MissioNexus and board member of the National Association of Evangelicals

"It is time for some creative correctives to some practices in present church planting movements, and encouragement as well. Wilson's work does both. We need a book like this."

TOM STEFFEN, Professor Emeritus of Intercultural Studies, Biola University, author of *Passing the Baton: Church Planting that Empowers* and *The Facilitator Era*

"Gene Wilson's *Emerging Gospel Movements: The Role of Catalysts* is likely to become the standard text in American seminaries for understanding contemporary gospel movements and the role that westerners can play in contributing to such movements. Based on twenty years of observing dozens of developing gospel movements throughout the world, the author concludes that both national leaders and the catalysts who come beside them have important roles to play."

DAVID R. DUNAETZ, Associate Professor Azusa Pacific University; Book Review Editor, *EMQ*; Editor, Great Commission Research Journal

"Have you seen God at work through your ministry? You may be on the launching pad for greater things. Can you envision going beyond your means and capacity by becoming an activator, a catalyst, a facilitator, a bridge person? Gene Wilson masterfully helps us see what our role could be in realizing emerging gospel movements. Read this book with an open heart, attuned to believing that God can use you to help foster a gospel movement."

DIETRICH SCHINDLER, Europe-wide Church Planting Consultant, author of *SHIFT: The Road to Level 5 Church Multiplication* and *The Jesus Model: Planting Churches the Jesus Way*

Emerging Gospel Movements

Emerging Gospel Movements

The Role of Catalysts

GENE WILSON

foreword by Steve Addison

WIPF *&* STOCK · Eugene, Oregon

EMERGING GOSPEL MOVEMENTS
The Role of Catalysts

Wipf & Stock
An Imprint of Wipf and Stock Publishers
199 W. 8th Ave., Suite 3
Eugene, OR 97401

www.wipfandstock.com

PAPERBACK ISBN: 978-1-6667-3007-4
HARDCOVER ISBN: 978-1-6667-2112-6
EBOOK ISBN: 978-1-6667-2113-3

Quotations from the Bible are from the New International Version, Copyright ©
1996 by Biblica, Inc.

11/30/21

Contents

List of Abbreviations

CIELB	Convenção das Igrejas Evangélicas Livres (Convention of Evangelical Free Churches)
CLC	Christian Literature Crusade
CMT	Church Multiplication Training
CPM	Church Planting Movement
DBS	Discovery Bible Study
DMM	Disciple-Making Movement
EFCA	Evangelical Free Church of America
EFCWA	Evangelical Free Church of West Africa
EMQ	Evangelical Missions Quarterly
FPG	Frontier People Group
IMB	International Mission Board (of the Southern Baptist Church)
ISFM	International Society for Frontier Missiology
LPN	Los Pinos Nuevos (The New Pines)
MBB	Muslim Background Believer
OMF	Overseas Missionary Fellowship
PMC	People Movement to Christ
SETIEL	Seminário Teológico nas Igrejas Evangélicas Livres (Evangelical Free Church Theological Seminary)
STM	Short-Term Mission
T4T	Training for Trainers
UPG	Unreached People Group

Foreword

Jesus founded something completely new in human history, a missionary move-ment intent on making disciples of every people group on earth. That is the core missionary task. The book of Acts is the story of how the Word spreads, grows, and multiplies. Wherever the gospel goes in the power of the Spirit, the fruit is disciples learning to follow Christ together in community.

In this generation, we have witnessed the proliferation of gospel move-ments around the world that multiply disciples and churches. Ten years ago, Justin Long thought there might be around one hundred multiplying movements of disciples and churches around the world. By 2017, he had documented six hundred movements—beyond all expectations.[1]

A movement consistently sees four generations of disciples gathered in churches, in multiple streams. Usually that's at least one thousand disciples, but the important measure is four generations of disciples and churches. Once a movement reaches four generations, it rarely ends. Today, Long is tracking 1,369 movements around the world, over 1 percent of the world's population, at least seventy-seven million disciples in 4.8 million churches. In addition, there are 4,500 *engagements* around the world. An engagement is a team or teams focused on starting a movement among a specific people group, cluster, or language. These movements are found predominantly in Asia and Africa, where the world's population is growing the fastest. The largest number of disciples are among former Muslims and Hindus. Long has also documented movements in Europe, Latin America, North Ameri-ca, and the Pacific.

There's no going back. Gospel movements that multiply disciples and churches are at the heart of the fulfilment of the Great Commission. That's why Gene Wilson's work is timely and important. The age of the missionary going out to plant and then lead a local church in an unreached field is over, although the practice continues. This is the era of emerging movements of

1. Long, "One Percent," 37–42.

xi

disciples among every people group throughout the world. This is the age of missionaries as catalysts for multiplying disciples and churches.

Wilson grounds his understanding of movement in the New Testament. He shows how Paul planted churches not as a sole pastor, but as a movement catalyst intent on reaching whole cities and regions before moving on to a new frontier. He has researched a dazzling array of both historical and contemporary case studies of movements—from India to China, from Cuba to Nicaragua, from the Muslim world to Europe and North America. He maps the characteristics of movements and the stages of their development. From his research and his field experience, Wilson lays out the qualities and functions of an effective movement catalyst, a role that is open to any nationality.

The future of the movement that Jesus started is to be found in those parts of the world where population growth is at its strongest. The West is no longer the center but is itself a mission field. This is the era of indigenous disciple-making movements across the globe reaching every tribe and tongue. Church-planting catalysts are a critical component of this advance.

STEVE ADDISON

Movement Catalyst and Director of MOVE
Author of *Movements That Change the World: Five Keys to Spreading the Gospel* (2009) and other books.[2]

2. See https://www.movements.net/steve/about-steve.

Preface

How This Book Came into Being

This book comes from twenty years of experience alongside developing movements. Throughout the world, God is transforming spiritual landscapes through leaders of *gospel movements* and the *catalysts* who come alongside them. This book is for all who long to be part of God's redemptive and transforming work among the nations.

A few questions keep coming up: "Why gospel movements?" "Are they just the latest missional fad?" "What do these movements have in common?" We will look at their shared qualities and notable differences. Others asked, "How do they get started?" and "What is exceptional about the initial disciples and churches?" Gospel movements are never static. They move through a series of growth stages. Most kingdom workers are not experiencing a full-blown movement. We want to help them assess the movement, and what is needed to move forward. So, we will look at the life process of movements, especially emergence factors.

And finally, people ask, "What can outsiders contribute to these emerging gospel movements?" At the encouragement of a teammate, I wrote the article "Church-Planting Catalysts for Gospel Movements," published by *Evangelical Missions Quarterly* and later posted online by *Christianity Today*. Since then, people have said that more is needed. Craig Ott, my friend and coauthor of *Global Church Planting: Biblical Principles and Best Practices for Multiplication* (Baker Academic, 2011), did the seminal work on the four stages of gospel movement maturity, providing an interpretive grid and a helpful pathway for movement catalysts.

We have observed dozens of movements up close and studied some in depth with special attention to their early development. This book is not limited to rapidly multiplying house churches. We look as well at more traditional types of churches that are multiplying because disciples and leaders are reproducing. Rather than focusing solely on rapid numeric growth, we chose criteria that reflect biblical values such as spiritual vitality, reproductive ministry, and life transformation.

This book is not about the biggest and best movements. We aim for an honest portrayal of movements we have known personally, examining spiritual factors, social dynamics, and human struggles. We identified five benchmarks to qualify a gospel movement for more in-depth research. These movements have

- grown numerically at a faster pace than the birth rate of the country they are in;

- grown qualitatively as evidenced by disciple and leader development;

- served their communities and seen lives transformed around them;

- reproduced churches across three generations or more;[1]

- and sent missionaries cross-culturally to unreached people groups.

An important clarification is in order. In this book we focus on external catalysts who come alongside indigenous or insider movement leaders to develop them and help them multiply churches. Others have studied qualities and have written profiles of the pioneering or apostolic leaders who launch and lead church planting movements.[2] In chapter 3 we explore the complementary roles of insider movements leaders and external movement catalysts.

Several colleagues advised and others helped with interviews, manuscript review, and editing. The use of "we" reflects that collaboration, although the author is fully responsible for the content. We used questionnaires to get the perspective of multiple leaders involved in each movement and followed up with personal interviews of one or more key leaders. The examples of movements and stories of catalysts are all real and accurate to the best of our knowledge. We asked the movement leaders to read the case studies and make corrections as needed. We have shared their analysis and evaluative comments in the case studies, except when the author's

---

1. We are focusing on emerging movements. This is not a definition of a full-fledged Church Planting Movement.

2. This type of movement leader is described in Addison 2019 and in Prinz 2021.

perspective is specified. Some asked us to conceal their real names for security reasons; others preferred that we use their real name.

I do not write as a movement-maker, but I have enjoyed being a coach and encourager to movement leaders. I report their stories and lessons learned from their vision, courage, and actions. They insisted that God receive all the glory. He is the only hero worthy of acclaim. I am grateful for the counsel of many in this project, in particular Craig Ott, Tom Steffen, Bob Logan, and Steve Addison. Shannon Alley provided invaluable editing. I am very thankful for the support and counsel of these friends, and many others. I dedicate this book to my dear wife, Linda, who has been my partner and inspiration in life and ministry for close to fifty years. None of this would have been possible without her.

Each chapter begins with New Testament foundations, identifies principles and best practices, and concludes with a representative story. Through interviews and questionnaires, dozens of people involved in gospel movements on five continents contributed insights to this book—men and women, lay people and professionals, teachers and evangelists, pastors and planters. The stories of God's redemptive grace through gospel movements will inspire and instruct. Our dream is to see many catalysts on mission with God, not working in isolation, but contributing together to new gospel movements. Thank you for joining us in this journey of discovery!

Introduction

Movement Catalysts Needed

God is raising up movement leaders all over the world and changing the spiritual landscape in places thought impenetrable to Christian witness. As a result, the gospel is no longer moving from west to east, or north to south, but from everywhere to everywhere, penetrating unreached peoples and piercing pockets of resistance.

At the same time, an increasing number of Christians from established churches are traveling abroad to help. Thousands of well-intentioned Christian business leaders, missionaries, pastors, and teachers travel overseas every year to contribute to gospel movements by bringing spiritual and material resources. At the height of the Short-Term Mission (STM) movement, an estimated 1.6 million young North American believers went abroad every year on STM trips.[1] These volunteers, who travel for Christ with good spiritual motives, often are over-confident but poorly informed. They lack discernment and have inadequate preparation and guidance. Though well-intentioned, they sometimes do more harm than good.

Oscar Muriu, pastor and leader of the Nairobi Chapel movement in Kenya, finds that "short term experiences have their place, but they need to be more carefully constructed. All too often a church says: 'We'd like to come for a short-term experience.' Then they say, in so many words, 'We're going to do A, B, C, D, and we're in charge.'"[2] On the other hand, Paul Gupta, from the Hindustan Bible Institute, welcomes those who "adjust their vision

---

1. MacDonald, "Sunshine Samaritans," para. 9.
2. Muriu, "African Planter," 97.

and redefine their role to partner with national churches."[3] He describes the type of contributor they encourage:

> But expatriates have an even greater role to play: Equipping thousands of these newly planted churches to be on mission with God. As a trainer, consultant, and facilitator, expatriates may serve the national church to develop a church-planting movement, or to equip that movement with the essential leadership skills and resources to grow mature, dynamic Christians and churches.[4]

We call those who contribute as Gupta suggests *catalysts*. In physics, catalysts are activators—small things that produce big results. Few people think much about them, but they are all around us. Whether chemicals or natural enzymes, they speed up a reaction and leverage change. In the long run, they save energy by reducing the amount of effort needed to create something new. Our daily life depends on them. Catalytic converters, Post-It Notes, laundry detergent, and beer all depend on catalysts, elements powerless in themselves, but effective when skillfully combined with other ingredients.

Human catalysts are change agents, not because they wield great power, but because they add just what is needed in the moment to produce desired change. They accelerate movement by injecting a critical element such as a partnership, training event, or timely challenge. They are *bridge people* who bring critical ideas, resources, and encouragement. They recognize that "although Western Christians may still have greater material and theological resources, non-Western Christians have much from which Western Christians can learn. We are stronger in mission together."[5]

Some are responding to this open door with enthusiasm, but without wisdom. Some transmit stagnant models of institutional church and programmatic ministry. They bring canned, resource-dependent strategies that create unhealthy dependencies. They are usually welcomed with open arms because of the social capital, resources, and connections they bring, but the partnership may only last while subsidies continue. This book presents an alternative: catalysts who prepare well, engage selectively, and contribute only what is needed, after listening well.

This book is intended to serve many—not only those from Western lands, but also those from developing nations. Church leaders who have invested thousands of dollars and ministry hours on mission teams wonder:

3. Gupta and Lingenfelter, *Breaking Tradition*, 198.
4. Gupta and Lingenfelter, *Breaking Tradition*, 198.
5. Ott, *Church on Mission*, 86.

"Where is this going? Should we continue?" An understanding of gospel movements and catalytic ministry will help them select priorities and steward resources.

This book will also provide direction to people like Carol, an experienced church planter, who recently had to leave Venezuela after helping to launch more church plants than any of our other missionaries in Latin America. As a single woman, she facilitated the planting of many churches, but lacked the confidence to serve as a catalyst on a broader scale. She could have invested in many more with some guidance. The missionary force is aging, and thousands of experienced workers, like Carol, are forced to leave their place of ministry because of health, family, or government restrictions. These valuable servants are not ready to be sent off to pasture. Some could serve for another decade by transitioning to a catalytic role.

Others will find their ministry enhanced through the principles and case studies in these pages. Several categories of cross-cultural or multiethnic workers will discover a pathway to facilitative ministry:

- medical professionals who can devote significant time abroad;

- pastors who love the Word and are passionate about helping others preach well;

- church planters who invest some of their time to develop another generation;

- men and women with business skills who could equip others with micro-business.

How about you? We are at a critical juncture in the fulfilment of the Great Commission. The end of the second millennium saw gospel movements emerge and extend in places where Christ was unknown. Today there are unique opportunities for churches and individuals who understand gospel movements to assist with wise investments. One need not have a success story to help others succeed. Like mundane scaffolding, catalysts come alongside and support emerging leaders in their kingdom work. But they have a vital role to play in the push to the finish line that Jesus describes: "And this gospel of the kingdom will be preached in the whole world as a testimony to all nations, and then the end will come" (Matt 24:14).

1

The Facilitator Era of Missions

Those who hear the word *catalyst* for the first time often raise a questioning eyebrow. Is this ministry biblical? Is it needed more now than in other periods of history? Tom Steffen, professor of missions at Biola University, answers in the affirmative to both questions, going so far as to call this period of history *the facilitator era* and *the fourth era of modern missions.*[1]

Why the fourth era? William Carey, pioneer in India, serves as a reference point for the first era of missions, *coastal missions*. Missionaries followed the European model of economic and political expansion by establishing beachheads in port cities. They gained a foothold along the coast, but rarely penetrated the interior where most of the unevangelized lived.

Hudson Taylor epitomizes the second era, *inland missions*. He left Shanghai and established a base in China's interior. Other American and Canadian missionaries followed, opening unexplored regions to the gospel at great personal cost. This pattern repeated itself in Africa and in other parts of Asia.

The third era of missions set its sights on *unreached peoples*. This era is best represented by two missionaries from the Student Volunteer Movement, Cameron Townsend, missionary to Guatemala and founder of Wycliffe Bible Translators, and Donald McGavran, missionary to India and missiologist in the Church Growth Movement. They wanted to reach eleven thousand unreached people groups (UPGs) with the gospel by the year

---

1. Steffen, *Facilitator Era*, 377.

2000.[2] The AD 2000 movement used the turn of the century to galvanize efforts and mobilize resources toward penetrating *every people group*.

While they did not fully realize those praiseworthy objectives, their efforts led to amazing missionary expansion. Thousands of UPGs have had Bible portions translated into their heart language and churches started in their midst. Countries like Korea, China, Nigeria, and Guatemala have seen the gospel penetrate many spheres of society and churches spread throughout the land. They, in turn, have set their sights on unreached peoples around them.

A NEW ERA IN MISSIONS?

Those who look back fifty years from now will decide whether this new missions paradigm warranted being called a new era of world missions. Only time will tell. But we are certainly living in a new day of opportunity. Former "mission fields" are now sending missionaries. In the beginning of the twentieth century, 82 percent of Christians lived in the global West and North, and missionaries from those Christianized regions went out to unreached people groups in the East and South.[3]

Now, in the twenty-first century, two-thirds of the world's Christians live in the Global South (Latin America, Africa, and Asia), and by 2050 that number is expected to grow to 77 percent.[4] Christians in these countries where the church is emerging have taken up the challenge of the UPGs at home and abroad. Missionaries from geographically and culturally distant lands can now partner with these new workers by serving as facilitators and catalysts. Renowned missiologist Paul Hiebert claims that these new realities create opportunities for *all* missionaries: "All missionaries now have a new role as 'in-betweeners.' They are bridge-persons, culture brokers, who stand between worlds and help each to understand the other. They stand between the church and unreached people and between churches and missions in different lands."[5]

This Facilitator Era offers great possibilities of cooperation through global technologies of connectedness (Internet, Zoom and WhatsApp). Partnerships in Great Commission ministry are being forged every day. For example, our team of Western catalysts is partnering with Indian nationals to reach Bhutanese, and with Nepalese to reach Tibetans. Other team

2. Winter and Hawthorne, "Four Men," B33–43.

3. Zurlo et al., "World Christianity 2020," 10.

4. Zurlo et al., "World Christianity 2020," 10.

5. Hiebert, *Gospel in Human Contexts*, 120.

members are partnering with Congolese and Liberians to evangelize people from sub-Saharan UPGs. These African believers, the fruit of second-era missionary efforts, are much more adept than Westerners at penetrating resistant places and reaching other African people groups.

Partnerships such as these have opened many doors. Catalytic ministry is occurring on an increasing scale. Multicultural teams and partnerships, while offering challenges, are also making headway in pluralistic cities. Trainers are taking theological and ministerial preparation *on the road* through modular courses and workshops. Experienced workers are using the web to coach the next generation.

Many of these *bridge-persons* contribute through biblical teaching and ministry training. But others are having an impact as well. Christian professionals, such as doctors and business consultants, enter countries closed to traditional missionaries. They leverage local ministry by using their know-how, resources, and relational capital. They add value to what local believers are doing but leave decision-making in their hands. Some will have the experience and gifting to enhance the local ministry rather than directing it.

> While some westerners will—and should—continue to enter pioneer church-planting roles in cross-cultural contexts, a growing majority will find other avenues to facilitate existing national church-planting movements in multiple ways. Some will facilitate the selection process of national church planters. Some will become involved in training nationals in theology, narrative, Bible translation, English, and missions.[6]

PRACTICAL BENEFITS OF CATALYTIC MINISTRY

This shift toward catalytic ministry has many advantages. Veterans who have labored in the front lines can use the wisdom gained over time and enjoy the privilege of investing in another generation of workers. They can assist by "equipping and mobilizing thousands in these newly planted churches to be on mission for God."[7] Their theological education, ministry experience, and personal maturity may qualify them as cross-cultural catalysts, when coupled with humility and cultural understanding.

Experienced church planters are having new opportunities to teach, coach, and facilitate church planting in other cultures. Culturally savvy veteran missionaries like Carol (see introduction) add value to national

6. Steffen, *Facilitator Era*, ii.
7. Gupta, *Breaking Tradition*, 98.

workers who have recently entered the missionary force. The modular training offered by visiting catalysts can mitigate the lack of formal training institutions in an under-evangelized region, if offered in their language and adapted to their learning style.

Two cautions are in order: First, catalytic ministry is not for everyone. It involves phasing in and out of relationships, challenging travel, constant learning, navigating expectations, avoiding dependency, and adapting to others, rather than having them adjust to you. Catalysts must be willing and able to relinquish control, step back from center stage, and allow local workers to take the lead. Some will not want to, and others, though willing, will struggle to make that shift.

The second caution is that those who have experienced fruitful ministries at home and want to help abroad may not be successful at bridging cultures. Some models and methods are not transferable. Effective catalysts teach principles and empower local believers to design their own culturally viable and sustainable ministries. Some cross-cultural experience and understanding of the receiving culture, religion, and worldview are critical (see chap. 9).

Catalytic ministry has its challenges, but the benefits outweigh them, if the vision is a gospel movement. Here is a summary (table 1.1):

Table 1.1
Benefits of Catalytic Ministry

For local people	*For the catalyst*
The ministry remains in the hands of local people.	Catalysts exert influence but do not take responsibility for the local ministry.
They are equipped in context without having to leave their jobs or ministries. The ministry is more likely to fit the context and be sustainable.	They learn from local believers wherever they go and can use that learning in other contexts.
They are exposed to new ideas, resources, and approaches.	They have the joy of investing in others through mentoring or coaching.
They observe in the catalyst a model of servant leadership that empowers others.	They gain a global perspective of God's work in the church and in the world.
	They can edify others through the accounts of resilience and perseverance in the face of poverty and persecution that they witness.

THE MAKING OF A CATALYST

I am not a movement-maker. However, I am learning to be a movement catalyst, and that is an awesome privilege. Catalysts are not experts. They are continual learners who believe that God wants to do more than we can ask or think (Eph 3:20). My wife and I journeyed from direct church planting to catalytic ministry in that spirit. After church planting for eighteen years in Quebec, Canada, God surprised us by taking us south to serve as church-planting coaches in Latin America. Based in the Miami region, we began to support and advance the efforts of missionaries and nationals in Latin America. My leaders asked me to mobilize church planting and develop church planters in ten Latin American countries. My first assignment was to assess and assist a Peruvian church planter, Ebdulio, in one of the poorest barrios of Lima, Peru.

For two solid days, I walked with him as he visited parishioners and neighbors in the streets. I ate with his family and slept in his home. On our last day together, he said to me, "You have spent more time with me than any of the Peruvian leaders or missionaries. Yet you have said nothing. Please tell me honestly what you think."

Ebdulio had a strong work ethic. He was personable, capable as an evangelist and teacher, and skilled at getting believers to join him in the work. He connected well with people in the community. The primary problem turned out to be a tactical one. He inherited a church building and assumed that church activities should take place there, even though few in the community were willing to enter a church building owned by *Evangélicos*.

When Ebdulio saw that the building was more of a handicap than stepping-stone, he shifted his focus to relational outreach in the barrio and developed small groups in homes. On my end, I learned that effective coaching begins with good observation. Catalysts may be eager to jump right in and problem-solve, but unless they have walked with the church planters and seen them in action, advice is premature, and may not be well-received.

While I was in Lima, I also taught a church-planting conference. To my dismay, only one church sent people to the event. To find out why, I made an appointment with each of the pastors and asked them when they planned to start a new church. Most offered excuses rather than plans.

The following year, one of the Peruvian pastors who had not previously participated, volunteered to host the training. I was pleased and intrigued. He explained his change of heart: "Last year, I wanted to hold on to *my* leaders. But the Lord made it clear: 'These are not *your* leaders. They are *mine*, and I will do with them whatever I please.'" Then he told his people, "Ask God how he wants you to serve, and we will get behind you. I pray he will call many of you into his harvest field." He hosted an energized group of learners from several churches.

I developed and taught an online church-planting course, facilitated gatherings of leaders, offered workshops, and visited church planters, but my central role was still unclear. At a coaching clinic, my trainer advised: "If you want to advance church planting in all those countries, you will need more than coaching. Yours is more of a director role." I clearly lacked the authority and resources to *direct* church planting across Latin America. My assignment was to serve as a *catalyst*, but the term was not yet being used.

As I traveled to other Latin American countries to assess and speak into their church-planting vision and efforts, I quickly realized that developing church planters required much more than occasional visits, conferences, or workshops. Our partners needed coaches on site in each country. Colleagues helped me design a plan for this. We offered a regional coaching clinic and asked each of our partner denominations to send an experienced church planter with the profile of a coach. These apprentice coaches met as a cohort once a year for three years.

The first time we were together, an apprentice coach asked, "How will we coach others when we have never been coached ourselves?" In response, I coached them for a year using Skype, as they were coaching church planters around them. The next year we met to share experiences and to strengthen our coaching ministries. Finally, the third year, we focused on best practices, training, and resources to develop another generation of planters.

My role evolved from organizer to facilitator, as they grew in knowledge and skill. Relationships grew and continue to this day. We worked on church-planting support systems (chap. 10) and developed a Spanish online resource bank. Several of them became church-planting catalysts for their association. We found that good things happen when leaders cooperate and learn from each other.

In 2009, our mission leaders asked me to develop and lead a global team of church-planting catalysts. Church-planting leaders from Africa, Asia, Europe, North America, and Latin America gathered in Orlando, Florida, at an Exponential Conference to learn, brainstorm, and build trusting relationships. For the last ten years, we have met as a virtual learning community and traveled together to advance gospel movements all over the world.

We are everyday people that God has graciously used to grow his global church, for reasons we do not fully understand. Our journey into catalytic ministry illustrates the power of collaboration. Most gospel movements do not come from exceptionalism—unique individuals, churches, or strategies—but from leaders who come together sacrificially to pool gifts and resources for a cause greater than themselves. In the process we are learning to:

- prioritize the spiritual dynamics, indigenous nature, and DNA of gospel movements;

- assess the stage of gospel movement maturity and engage appropriately;

- take the posture of a catalyst to develop and empower movement leaders;

- develop best practices to be effective in catalytic ministry;

- grow the personal qualities needed to be a fruitful catalyst;

- select other catalysts in which to invest.

In what follows, we will examine gospel movements to discover preferred pathways of facilitative ministry that contribute to transformation and multiplication. Those who have documented Christian movements have primarily focused on exceptional contemporary cases. Some have reviewed historical accounts and drawn principles from them. Addison (2011) shows that five elements found in movements throughout history were also central to Jesus' ministry. But few, if any, have started with a biblical lens and built up from a biblical foundation. The book of Acts is more than a historical account. It is a repository of patterns and principles for gospel movements today. This will become evident in the exciting story of the first gospel movements.

2

Gospel Movements in the New Testament and Today

"*All over the world* this gospel is bearing fruit and growing, just as it has been doing among you since the day you heard it and understood God's grace in all its truth" (Col 1:6). This could be said of the twenty-first century as well as the first. We hear wonderful reports of gospel movements where for years the spiritual terrain was arid, rocky, and seemingly impenetrable.

WHAT DO WE MEAN BY GOSPEL MOVEMENTS?

Movement can refer to a growing fellowship of like-minded churches or a cause that spreads beyond its place of origin. However, we are talking about the kind of gospel movement found in Acts, the kind that takes place when the gospel penetrates, transforms, and multiplies disciples on a significant scale. Those movements, propelled by the gospel, can look very different externally but they share a common core we will explore as we move forward.

A Christian movement called Focus on Fruit (FoF) is growing in Pulao, a Malaysian island with a Muslim majority. Frank Preston found that, by 2014, FoF had grown to about 7,500 Muslim-background believers (MBBs) in three disciple-making chains of reproduction called "streams."

> Currently FoF has documented an excess of 12,944 churches comprising of five or more Muslim background believers per church with twenty-five local activists *(apostles)* reaching into

forty Muslim Unreached People Groups in twelve countries. The leadership structure has three key local leaders and about fifteen stream leaders.[1]

A very different gospel movement called "The Way" started in Jerusalem in the first century. These two gospel movements look very different but have two essentials in common: the gospel and a movement DNA.

Gospel movements—The first operative word, "gospel," reminds us that the good news of Jesus, empowered by the Holy Spirit, propels these movements, bringing new life and transformation. "The whole life of the church should be characterized by witness to the kingdom of God and the transformative power of the gospel of Jesus Christ."[2] Gospel movements put the good news of Jesus front and center, as the irreplaceable power to deliver and transform people. It is the only life source, the only truth that sets people free and starts them a new journey with the living Christ. When the truth of the gospel is adulterated or sidelined, movements sputter and die. Faithfulness to the gospel must be guarded at any price.

- Gospel movements are *evangelical* (pertaining to and rooted in the *evangel* or gospel) and recognize these four truths as bulwarks of gospel-centered teaching and hallmarks of Evangelical faith:

- *Sola Scriptura*—Scripture alone. The Bible is the only authority for Christian life and belief.

- *Solo Cristo*—Christ alone. Jesus Christ is the only mediator between God and people.

- *Sola Gratia*—Grace alone. Salvation is a gift of God's grace, never earned through human works or religious practice.

- *Sola Fide*—Faith alone. Salvation is received by faith alone, not through the sacraments, meritorious actions, or religious activities.

The second operative word, "movement," speaks of the missional and multiplicative nature of the church. Keller warns, "It is common for Christian ministries, indeed for human organizations, to claim to be a movement. It has a very positive ring to contemporary ears. When Christians use the term, they often mean, 'God is blessing our efforts.'"[3]

But gospel movements are characterized by centrifugal motion. God's redeemed people, obedient to the Great Commission, are never static but

---

1. Preston, "Scripture Engagement," para. 3.

2. Ott, *Church on Mission*, 35.

3. Keller, "Defining Gospel Movement."

always on the move with their Lord, making, maturing, and multiplying disciples. In this book, *movement* describes the collective advance of fellowships of Christ-followers that multiply over several generations. These churches, propelled by the Holy Spirit and the Word, reproduce geographically, numerically, and generationally, forming regional constellations of cooperating churches that, in turn, cross new frontiers, and transform entire societies.

> So as the church preaches the gospel to individuals, three things happen. Nominal Christians (people who think of themselves as Christians but have not been spiritually born again) get converted. Sleepy Christians (people who are believers, but their lives show little of the power and fruit of the Spirit) wake up. And non-Christians—lots of them—start getting attracted and converted, because Christians are more willing and able to engage them and show them the beauty of Christ . . . The greater the number of individuals changed, the greater the gospel movement. There is a great variety. Gospel movements can be in a single church or across a whole continent or continents.[4]

Gospel movements are not a uniquely modern phenomenon, they form the backdrop of Luke's narrative in Acts and can be found in many periods of church history. They are essentially Jesus movements—Christocentric movements that manifest who Jesus is, what he did on the cross, and what he is doing through his Spirit and church because of the resurrection.

NEW TESTAMENT GOSPEL MOVEMENTS

The gospel movement that started in Galilee exploded in Jerusalem, extended into neighboring Samaria, and took hold in Syrian Antioch. From there, it gave birth to multiple cross-cultural movements that turned the world upside down. Spirit-filled apostles and lay witnesses spread the Word onward and outward, penetrating all the pagan centers of the Roman Empire, so that the church had grown to an estimated forty thousand Christians by the year AD 150.[5] Figure 2.1 illustrates this outward movement of church multiplication.

4. Keller, "Defining Gospel Movement."

5. Stark, *Rise of Christianity*, 7.

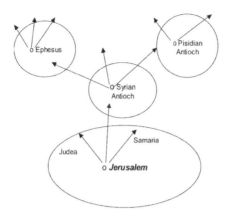

New Testament Gospel Movements

The Way: A Judean Gospel Movement

The New Testament gospel movements are not separate, but vitally connected branches of the same movement, initially called "the Way."[6] Jesus modeled what he sent out his disciples to do—make disciples (Matt 28:18–20). He showed his rightful authority as Messiah through miracles and sent his disciples to find households of peace that would receive the good news. First, he sent twelve, then seventy-two, and finally, an even larger company of disciples (Luke 9, 10, and 24:33–49). From those modest beginnings, the gospel spread broadly throughout Judea, to Samaria, and eventually into the Gentile world.

The movement was *intentional and expanded progressively* as Jesus' disciples developed other followers. Between the Feast of the Tabernacles and the Passover of his final year, Jesus taught his disciples privately and prepared them for what was to come. They scattered when he was taken, scourged, and hung on a cross. After he came back to life, and appeared to them repeatedly, they rallied with renewed hope. One hundred twenty believers gathered in the upper room to pray (Acts 1:15), and later, at his ascension, around five hundred met, most likely in Galilee (Matt 28:7, 16; 1 Cor 15:6).

On the day of Pentecost, the apostles were filled with the Holy Spirit, and those who had fled for their lives earlier, now risked all to make Jesus

6. This expression referred to the faith and manner of life of followers of Jesus and seems to be used primarily by people outside the fold (Acts 9:2; 19:9, 23; 22:4, 14; 24:22).

known. Miracles and bold preaching drew many to the risen Lord. The common people held the believers in high esteem, although the religious authorities saw them as a threat (Acts 5:11–18). Crowds brought their sick and demon-possessed to be healed and delivered (Acts 5:16).

Three thousand were added to the church in response to Peter's Pentecost message but, after that, "the Lord added to their number *daily* those who were being saved" (Acts 2:47, my emphasis added). As a result, about ten thousand people (five thousand men plus women and children) chose to follow the Galilean named Jesus (Acts 4:4). The message they shared, reinforced by their good reputation and corporate witness, fueled this growth. According to one historian, "one of the most important methods of spreading the gospel in antiquity was by the use of homes . . . Christian missionaries made a deliberate point of gaining whatever households they could as lighthouses, so to speak, from which the gospel could illuminate the surrounding darkness."[7]

Peter and Phillip took the good news to Judea and Samaria, respectively. As a result, "the church throughout Judea, Galilee, and Samaria enjoyed a time of peace. It was strengthened; and encouraged by the Holy Spirit, grew in numbers, living in the fear of the Lord" (Acts 9:31). The expression "grew in numbers" is "multiplied" in the original Greek. The growth drew opposition and the believers enjoyed peace for only five years. Claudius became emperor and Herod Agrippa tried to impress him by beheading James and imprisoning Peter.[8]

Stephen was stoned and the church dispersed, fleeing violent persecution. The apostles took a lower profile, teaching the newly converted only in homes. Until Constantine proclaimed the Edict of Milan in 313, the household was the basic gathering unit of the church and force behind its mission.[9]

Despite Stephen's murder, the movement was not lost, for "those who had been scattered preached the Word wherever they went" (Acts 8:4). Luke describes the rapid numerical and maturational gains of this Judean movement in terms of strengthening and multiplication (Acts 9:31; 12:24). Up to this point, the Way was an ethnically Jewish movement, but this was soon to change.

7. Green, *Evangelism Early Church*, 210.

8. Bruce, *Acts*, 246–47.

9. Meeks, *First Urban Christians*, 75–76.

Syrian Extension

Antiochian Jews who came to faith in Jerusalem at Pentecost fled persecution and returned to the relative anonymity of Syrian Antioch—a multicultural population forming the third largest city in the world. Later, believers from Cyprus and Cyrene joined them and began to speak to Greeks and Jews about Jesus. "The Lord's hand was with them, and a great number of people believed and turned to the Lord" (Acts 11:21). As a result, the first mixed Jewish and Gentile church emerged.

When Barnabas went to see what was happening, there was another great ingathering. Barnabas and Paul taught great numbers of people for an entire year. Antioch became home to the largest number of followers of the Way outside of Jerusalem. This diverse and dynamic fellowship, led by a multi-gifted international team of prophets and teaching elders, became a model of missionary sending and church-based training. The Holy Spirit directed the Antiochian church to send Barnabas and Saul even farther with the gospel. *The Way* was now a cosmopolitan movement, not a strictly Jewish sect, and the name "Christian"—belonging to Christ—reflected this change.

The Antioch church also served as a bridge between Jerusalem and the Gentile mission. She championed outreach to Gentiles and advocated freedom from Jewish legal impositions. She became the *anchor church* of westward expansion and provided a pattern for missionary extension—teams of elders for newly planted churches and teams of missionaries to start new ones. The apostolic teams replicated both practices as they crossed frontiers with the gospel (Acts 14:23).

From Antioch, Paul and Barnabas first went to two regions familiar to them: Cyprus and Pisidia. Despite much opposition, "the Word of the Lord spread through the whole region" (Acts 13:49), and "a great number of Jews and Gentiles believed" (14:1). At the close of this venture, they returned to Antioch, reported all God had done, and remained for a while in their sending church.

Multiplication in Thessalonica

On the second missionary journey (Acts 15:40—18:22) Paul and his companions traveled north, through Syria, Cilicia, and Pisidia, strengthening the churches. After being sent to Greece by means of a vision, they preached the gospel in Philippi, Thessalonica, Berea, Athens, and Corinth. The work in Thessalonica illustrates how a gospel movement goes from *pioneer planting* to *local multiplication*.

Although Paul initially stayed in Thessalonica for only three weeks, he sent Timothy to strengthen and encourage them in their faith (1 Thess 3:2). Paul and his friends returned briefly to encourage and equip the local disciples but expected them to continue the work. We have no record of how the churches grew in Berea, Philippi, and Athens. However, the new Thessalonian believers powerfully influenced the entire Greek peninsula and beyond, as Paul affirms: "The Lord's message rang out from you, not only in Macedonia and Achaia—your faith in God has become known everywhere" (1 Thess 1:8).

Later, during his third missionary journey, Paul "traveled through that area, speaking many words of encouragement to the people" (Acts 20:2). He also spent some time in Thessalonica on his return trip, picking up Aristarchus and Secundus, workers from that city who brought the funds they had collected for the poor in Jerusalem (Acts 20:4).

Ephesian and Corinthian Movements

Paul and his associates moved back and forth between two strategic cities, Corinth and Ephesus. The apostle stayed in Corinth a year and a half after God assured him that a harvest remained (Acts 18:9–10). Then he went to Ephesus and, after a brief preaching ministry in the synagogue, turned things over to his colleagues Priscilla and Aquila. The couple mentored Apollos, and together, they discipled an initial group of Ephesian believers (Acts 18:19–26).

Then Apollos moved to Corinth and Paul returned to Ephesus where he led the effort to multiply disciples. He stayed there two additional years, teaching in a hall called the *School of Tyrannus*, "so that all the Greeks and Jews who lived in the Province of Asia heard the word of the Lord" (Acts 19:10). After dramatic conversions of demon-possessed people and sorcerers, "the name of the Lord Jesus was held in high honor" (18:17) and "the word of the Lord spread widely and grew in great power" (18:20).

To understand how the Ephesian church became a movement, we must look closely at Paul's message to the elders of that church (Acts 20:18–35). We learn that, besides the initial teaching in the *School of Tyrannus*, he taught and trained disciples in homes and in public (Acts 20:20), and for three years he mentored those who would become elders (Acts 20:31). Several daughter churches emerged (1 Cor 16:19).

Since, according to the record in Acts, Paul did not plant other churches in the Lycus valley around Ephesus, those he discipled must have planted
the daughter churches mentioned in the book of Revelation. A disciple from
the region, Epaphras, started the daughter church in Colossae (Col 1:7) and
probably those in Laodicea and Hierapolis as well (Col 4:12–13).

Paul hoped that the Corinthian church would, like Ephesus, become
a sending base for missionaries to unreached people groups beyond it. On
his third missionary journey, he returned there for three months to strength
the work and prepare them to send missionaries (Acts 20:2). He writes to
the Corinthians, "Our hope is that, as your faith continues to grow, our area
of activity among you will greatly expand, so that we can preach the gospel
in the regions beyond you" (2 Cor 10:15–16). He envisioned missionary-
sending churches that would reproduce regionally so that he could pioneer
in unevangelized territory, since he preferred to preach where Christ was
unknown (Rom 15:20).

CHARACTERISTICS OF GOSPEL
MOVEMENTS FROM THE BOOK OF ACTS

We should make a few observations at this point. They are gospel-centered
works of the Holy Spirit, birthed in prayer, that advance as his people reproduce disciples and churches across generations and geographical frontiers.
When they reach maturity, they are indigenous, grassroots movements,
meaning that the forces and resources that shape them are locally generated,
rather than imported from other places. Because of this, they are sustainable
and resilient, even in times of persecution.

They stand out because of the spiritual temper and qualities of their
disciples and leaders, rather than the strength of their strategies and methods. The pace of their growth is less important than the manner of their
growth. Indeed, movement development is influenced by many factors,
including external ones. But they have a common dynamic. Disciples make
other disciples, leaders mentor new leaders, and churches reproduce as a result. This multiplicative DNA, at the heart of gospel movements, constitutes
the primary dividing line between them and other types of movements and
associations.

This Spirit-led extension by reproduction was no franchising operation. These early movements were living works of God, not identical clones.
The apostles did not try to duplicate what happened at Pentecost or in Syrian Antioch. They consistently obeyed the Lord's Great Commission and
developed disciples in such a way that they too became collaborators in

future harvests. The following list shows that, although gospel movements share a common core, they have diverse emergence patterns—reflecting the Great Designer's power and creativity.

- Spontaneous cellular reproduction—early Jerusalem (Acts 2–7)

- Dispersion through migration—later Jerusalem (Acts 8–12)

- Saturation through itinerant proclamation—Pisidian Antioch (Acts 13:13—14:28)

- Pioneer work followed by local multiplication—Thessalonica (Acts 17; 1 Thess 1–2)

- Intentional disciple making and church planting by training workers—Corinth and Ephesus (Acts 18–20)

This diversity should be a word of caution to those who, having seen a movement launched in one context, conclude that all movements should use the same methods and tactics. The common pattern is gospel-sharing leading to reproducing disciples, leaders, churches, and missionaries. Finally, gospel movements grow both numerically and qualitatively. They transform while they expand. This is not only strategically wise; it is simply what the gospel does. Like the tiny mustard seed that becomes a big tree, in which many birds nest (Matt 13:31), the gospel ushers more and more people out of darkness into the light. As it does, it produces transformation like yeast working through a lump of dough (v. 32). The gospel converts people, brings healing to families, and leaves its mark on entire communities. This twofold work—expansion and transformation—is recorded time and time again in Acts. In the verses that follow, note the juxtaposition of transformation growth and expansion growth.

> ". . . praising God and enjoying the *favor of all the people*. And the *Lord added to their number* daily those who were being saved." (2:47)

> "Then the church throughout Judea, Galilee and Samaria enjoyed a time of peace. *It was strengthened*. And encouraged by the Holy Spirit, *it grew in numbers*, living in the fear of the Lord." (9:31)

> "So the churches *were strengthened* in the faith and *grew daily in numbers*." (16:5)

These two dimensions of church growth should not be set one against the other. There is a symbiotic relationship between them, although one does not necessarily follow the other. When held in balance, they are complementary and work synergistically to advance Christ's reign.

> In keeping with the Great Commission, if the world is to be reached with the gospel, and if transformational churches are to be established among every people and in every community, then disciples, leaders, ministries, and churches will need to be reproduced in ways that naturally can lead to further multiplication. In this sense methods and approaches to ministry that both qualitatively and quantitatively have the potential to multiply are a practical necessity.[10]

Missional movements characterized by biblically-sound disciples, leaders, and ministries will experience growth in God's time. Unhealthy movements will eventually stagnate or self-destruct. Some movements experience rapid growth, sustained over an extended period. But these church-planting movements (hereafter CPMs) are the exception rather than the rule. In Central America, for example, multiple gospel movements of modest but steady growth have won a higher percentage of people over fifteen years than did a full-fledged CPM (see chap. 4).

In Acts we learn that God used movements of different shape and scope. When it comes to gospel movements, one size does not fit all. Throughout this book, we will see that he continues to do so in this generation. This should be an encouragement to those working in the early stages of movement development and a caution to others who prescribe a narrow, methodological approach.

GOSPEL MOVEMENTS TODAY

Before jumping into distinctions between movements, it's important to acknowledge the limitations of this book. We humbly build on the research and writing of movement missiologists like David Garrison, David Watson, Steve Smith, Steve Addison, and others who have written about movements of God. As such, this book is an additional deposit and invitation to further study. We offer a part of the puzzle to inspire and help those who, like us, long to see gospel movements blossom, grow, and sprout other movements.

The rise of majority world missions—described in the preceding chapter—has largely been the fruit of gospel movements. At this writing, the *24:14 Coalition*, an umbrella group of CPM organizations, has gathered data on over one thousand movements. It is not possible to create a typology

---

10. Ott, *Church on Mission*, 104.

that would categorize all movements. However, what we know today comes from the New Testament and from the confluence of three streams of research and writing. Let's look at those streams in chronological order.

People Movements to Christ

The first source of movement understanding came in the mid-nineteenth century when mission leaders observed and reported on group conversions, later called "people movements to Christ" (PMC). They occurred when entire communities made "multi-individual, mutually interdependent decisions" to follow Jesus Christ.[11] These group conversions started when a family that was transformed by the gospel took a bold stand for Christ and shared their reasons with others.

Previously, initial converts had often been separated from their families and friends for their protection and spiritual nurture. Sometimes they were even taken to live in missionary compounds. But when they remained in their communities as living witnesses, despite ostracism and persecution, they often became *bridges of God* to their loved ones.

"Members of the close-knit group seek to persuade their loved ones of the great desirability of believing on Jesus Christ and becoming Christians."[12] These converts who stayed with their families communicated in their birth language, using cultural means that were meaningful to their peers. As a result, others came to Christ without having to cross linguistic and cultural boundaries. They could become Christians without betraying their loved ones. Then often entire families, clans, and tribes followed their brave example. McGavran was an avid student of the factors contributing to the receptivity of people movements. He found that some PMC movements require years, in some cases decades, of gospel exposure before they begin.[13] Although Roland Allen describes the emergence of PMC movements as "spontaneous expansion," most were preceded by a *gestation period.*

However, in a second stage, when missionaries relinquished control and empowered national evangelists to take the lead, local multiplication took place. The gospel traveled through kinship relationships at a more rapid pace. Mass baptisms of new Christ-followers gave testimony to the effective ministry of the local evangelists and preachers, prepared, and sent out by their missionary mentors. This approach of gospel infiltration and

---

11. McGavran, *Understanding Church Growth*, 302.

12. McGavran, *Understanding Church Growth*, 303.

13. McGavran, *Understanding Church Growth*, 216–32.

group conversion still occurs in some close-knit societies and in rural animistic groups.

Methods and means are not neutral, they color the gospel in the eyes of the beholder. The cultural soil and social structure of the people affect the way people respond to the gospel. Obstacles are not only religious; they are sociological as well. An approach that appears foreign and imposed will rarely lead to an emerging movement. On the other hand, evangelism and discipleship that are congruent with the culture will more often open doors and allow the gospel to spread and transform. The stage is set for multiplication when people do not have to betray their culture or identify with a foreign religious system to believe in Jesus and follow him.

Church Planting Movements

David Garrison wrote the classic work on CPMs, defining them and describing what they have in common and what hinders their development. For almost thirty years he was a Southern Baptist missionary, working alongside Indian nationals from several tribes. He observed the evangelists who gave birth to movements and documented the patterns that contributed to multiplicative growth. Garrison studied a dozen languages and served as global strategist for the International Missions Board (IMB). His PhD in history and extensive travel (one hundred countries), give him a unique perspective and wise caution. He avoids prescribing from one culture what should be done in others. He considers the common elements of CPMs descriptive, not prescriptive.

1. Extraordinary Prayer

2. Abundant Evangelism

3. Intentional Planting of Reproducing Churches

4. The Authority of God's Word

5. Local Leadership

6. Lay Leadership

7. House Churches

8. Churches Planting Churches

9. Rapid Reproduction

10. Healthy Churches[14]

14. Garrison, *Church Planting Movements*, 172.

CPMs are defined as a "rapid multiplication of indigenous churches planting other churches that sweeps through a people group or population segment."[15] Note the words "rapid" and "sweeps." CPMs stand out by their rapid and exponential reproduction, producing explosive growth. Two colleagues of Garrison, David Watson and Steve Smith, have added to our understanding of CPMs from their work as strategy coordinators with the IMB, Watson in India and Smith in China. Both have taken a more prescriptive stand, identified patterns that help a CPM advance, and devised a strategic pathway based on their discoveries.

Disciple-Making Movements (David Watson)

David Watson began the Disciple-Making Movements (DMM) effort with a team of five Indian nationals, among the Bhojpuri of Northern India, an area known as the graveyard of missions and missionaries. It took two years to see the first church born from their disciple-making efforts. Watson recounts, "All of a sudden, we saw eight churches planted in one year. The next year, there were 48 new churches planted. The year after that, 148, then 327, and then 500. In the fifth year, we saw more than 1,000 new churches planted!"[16] Watson calls movements like this one DMMs because they are the fruit of intentional disciple making. "In our experience a CPM is the result of obedience-based discipleship that see disciples reproducing disciples, leaders reproducing leaders and churches reproducing churches—in other words a Disciple-Making Movement."[17]

Initially, evangelists find *people of peace*—those who welcome the messenger and listen to the message (Matt 10; Luke 10). The ones who profess faith, and give evidence of new life, are trained to disciple others and be part of a disciple-making congregation using discovery Bible study (DBS) groups. These groups reproduce, creating streams of new disciples. Multiplication takes place at all levels as members share the Bible narratives and start new groups. New churches are the outcome of these disciple-making streams. They are applying these principles among some of the marginalized groups in North America, and, although they have not seen explosive growth, hundreds of DBS groups have taken root in fourteen states.

15. Garrison, *Church Planting Movements*, 21.

16. Watson, *Contagious Disciple Making*, xiii.

17. Watson, *Contagious Disciple Making*, 6.

Training for Trainers Movements (Steve Smith and Ying Kai)

Steve and Laura Smith served as missionaries in East Asia for eighteen years. Since 2013, they have worked globally to catalyze gospel movements with several organizations. They were involved in a CPM among a previously unreached people group in Asia with Ying and Grace Kai, a Taiwanese pastoral couple. Ying and Grace responded to God's call to "train trainers" in mainland China. They began with an initial meeting of thirty Christians. Half of them had never shared their faith, but all were equipped and became accountable to witness and disciple others.[18] The marvelous movement that resulted produced more than forty thousand new churches and half a million new believers. Their discipleship training is structured, simple, and reproducible. Disciple makers hold each other accountable in groups.

Garrison reminds us that there are no passengers in CPMs. Everyone is part of the labor force. In that spirit, T4T is a tool used to mobilize and prepare followers of Jesus to disciple the people in their oikos (relational network). T4T integrates evangelism, discipleship, church planting, and leadership development. It starts with the saved and equips them to move out with the gospel, while DMM generally begins with pre-Christians in their natural environment.

Together Smith and Kai wrote *T4T: A Discipleship Re-revolution*, detailing the biblical principles behind CPMs and a process developed by Kai and his wife to pursue such movements. T4T movements really take off when all Christians accept the call to be disciple makers and members of a church-planting team.

There is broad agreement, despite divergent strategies, that these three types of movements (PMC, DMM, and T4T) are gospel movements that become CPMs at their apex.[19] One could say that CPMs are gospel movements *on steroids*. In Jesus' parable of the sower (Matt 13), CPMs would be the bumper crop that produces one hundred times the grain used. Or they could be compared to powerful waves that suddenly and significantly change the spiritual landscape, signs of God's gracious intervention at a critical moment in history. They fascinate us, lift our spirits, capture our imagination, and remind us of God's power. Although exceptional in scope and pace, they have much in common with other gospel movements. Fervent prayer and evangelism give birth to streams of disciples making disciples, resulting in generations of reproducing churches. The chart below

---

18. Garrison, *Church Planting Movements*, 286–93.

19. A more detailed comparison and contrast between these three types of CPMs is included in appendix 1.

(table 2.1) illustrates why CPMs are gospel movements but not all gospel movements are CPMs.

Table 2.1

Church-Planting Movements and Gospel Movements

Church-Planting Movements	Gospel Movements
A rapid multiplication of indigenous churches planting churches that sweeps through a people group or population segment.	An advance of Jesus' kingdom (reign) through the spread of the gospel and the generational multiplication of disciples and churches within a demographic group.
Rapid, exponential numeric growth of churches. Four or more generations of church reproduction. Healthy churches.	Spiritual vitality and transformative growth (discipleship and leadership) that lead to generations of church multiplication.
Home-based churches led by local leaders who are not theologically trained (lay people).	Churches of various types and sizes that reproduce consistently because disciples do. Some are led by pastors, others by lay people.
CPMs are often the climax and culmination of a gospel movement.	Gospel movements start with a modest pace of reproduction but accelerate and may become a CPM; but not all do.

In CPMs the period of rapid growth lasts for a while, even decades, but eventually levels off. The leveling-off can be the product of negative factors like conflict, the loss of passion, moral failure of the founder, or false teaching. But it can also come from natural factors like the need for leadership growth to catch up to discipleship multiplication. In some cases, the plateau is beneficial and leads to another wave of growth.

CPMs usually emerge in exceptional times—as in the wake of the devastation of the Khmer Rouge in Cambodia, in the vacuum created when Russia abandoned Cuba, or in the seismic changes that followed the fall of the Soviet Empire. These mega movements appear most frequently in rural, collectivistic societies, with tightly knit extended families and group decision making by elders, rarely in Western individualistic societies. "It appears the majority of movements began in rural areas and continue to operate mostly in those situations. Even when they are present in towns and cities, many of these areas have a rural flavor."[20] Why is this?

---

20. Long, "One Percent," 41.

We think this is because rural societies are much less complex than urban societies, and that just a few tactics are needed to start churches in these rural structures. When we look at the urban churches in our work, they are among village people who have moved to the city. So, basically, the same rural tactics are being used in the city, and are reaching migrant populations, but not traditional urbanites.[21]

Although CPMs are exceptional, less spectacular gospel movements are taking place all over the world. Long concurs: "However, generally speaking, most movements are in the size range of 1,000 to 10,000 people; a handful of movements are larger than one million members."[22]

We find gospel movements in every major geographic region of the world, except the Arctics, as seen by Long's research and the examples in this book.[23] The diversity of environments in which they grow should be an encouragement to those who do not experience an exceptional CPM or work in settings where rapid and exponential multiplication is not likely to take place. The very exceptionalism that causes CPMs to amaze us, should warn us against trying to replicate them uncritically. It should also keep us from assuming growth will continue at that rate. The explosive rate is only a stage of the movement (more in chapter 6).

AN EARLY MOVEMENT AMONG
SPIRIT WORSHIPPERS

Some advocates portray gospel movements as something entirely new. This is a fallacy. Gospel movements, some with CPM dimensions, are found in Acts and have occurred in history, especially since the early 1900s. Before that, in the early colonial era, missionary efforts were dominated by Westerners. Indigenous movements were rare during the colonial period. Gustav Warneck, the first university chair of missiology at Halle, Germany (1896–1908), stated, "Until today apart from the negro churches in the United States, there is no really independent native Christian church, that is, one wholly free from missionary supervision."[24]

This tragic situation began to change when the government forced missionaries to leave China. Some went to neighboring Korea, where they

21. Watson, *Contagious Disciple Making*, 31–32.

22. Long, "One Percent, 39.

23. Long, "One Percent," 39–41.

24. Warneck, *History of Missions*, 403.

applied indigenous church growth principles. The idea that expansion, financial support, and leadership should come from local Christians within the movement led to a wave of evangelism, discipling and church development by local men and women empowered by the Holy Spirit. Of course, that implied missionaries from colonial nations would relinquish control, and, in this case, they did.

A beautiful gospel movement emerged in Korea. "From the start the work was self-propagating, self-supporting, and self-governing, growing in four years from one church with ninety-three members to 153 churches with a total of 8,500 members and adherents."[25] Entire people groups were transformed by the gospel during this period, decades before the work on CPMs was penned.

John L. Nevius helped to launch this movement while only spending a couple weeks in Korea. He helped the new team of missionaries by providing form and focus to their work. He taught that churches should be shaped by local culture, led by local leaders, and supported by local funds. He guided the missionary team to prepare local workers and train them in the Word. He was a movement catalyst who helped the team facilitate the ministry of Koreans rather than leading the work themselves. This required a shift in strategy and a new ministry posture—missionaries as facilitators rather than directors.

J. O. Fraser was another pioneer who became a catalyst. He worked among the Lisu people of southwest China, an animistic people that believed in many spirit gods and lived under demonic oppression. Fraser, a single man at the time, initially traveled from village to village learning the language and telling them about the one true God. He preached and witnessed for several years with little fruit. Early converts kept falling back into the bondage of sin and spiritism. Then, in 1916, he and fellow missionaries started to see scores of families come to Christ and be set free from the grip of spirits that had previously bound them. What changed? His wife explains:

> He described to me how in his early years he had been all but defeated by the forces of darkness arrayed against him . . . He came to the place where he asked God to take away his life rather than to allow him to labor on without results. He would then tell me of the prayer forces that took up the burden at home and the tremendous lifting of the cloud over his soul, of the gift of faith that was given him and how God seemed suddenly to step in, drive back the forces of darkness and take the field.[26]

25. Ott and Wilson, *Global Church Planting*, 69.

26. Fraser, *Fraser and Prayer*, 11–12.

The cloud was lifted after Fraser did two things. He received grace himself, despite his weakness, to believe and pray the *prayer of faith* for several hundred Lisu families to come to Christ. He also recruited a prayer team to intercede specifically and regularly for the work. They fought the spiritual battle with him from a distance. These two changes produced a turning point and, in the years that followed, a gospel movement involving tens of thousands.

Along with prayer, intentional discipling propelled the movement forward. Missionaries developed a Lisu alphabet that is still in use today, translated Scripture, and taught them what it means to follow Jesus. They also helped the Lisu develop indigenous prayers and hymns. One of those prayers goes, "God, our Father, Creator of heaven and earth, Creator of mankind, we are your children. We are followers of Jesus. Watch over us this day. Don't let the evil spirits see us. Trusting in Jesus, Amen."[27]

It is important to realize the important but limited role of Fraser and his colleagues. They were itinerant evangelists who birthed the movement through prayer and persistent gospel sowing. Not until 1922 did any missionaries live among the Lisu. Influenced by Roland Allen's writing on Pauline church-planting and indigenous principles, Fraser had Lisu believers join him on evangelistic trips to unreached villages. The conviction that the Holy Spirit would work through new believers led him to pass the baton to Lisu evangelists without unnecessary delay, as reported by one of his colleagues:

> When the Lisu wanted to take the Gospel to their fellow tribesmen, Fraser encouraged them to go right ahead and exhorted those left behind to support the evangelists . . . Self-governance impacted the sending of evangelists. While a missionary might suggest where evangelism should be done (in part, because they were more aware of the wider needs), the churches would decide who would go, where they would go, and how much the evangelists would be paid. Prayer, itinerant evangelism, the Bible in their language, hymnody, and three-self principles can all be cited as things that led to the growth of the Lisu church.[28]

The use of local evangelists and church planters allowed the young movement to expand. Fraser was an amazing catalyst, known for his ability to organize the people into strong indigenous churches that became models for church-planting ventures. By 1918, nine years after he arrived in Yunnan

27. McConnell, "Mission to the Lisu," 31.

28. McConnell, "Mission to the Lisu," 32–33.

province, six hundred believers were baptized because of the work of local evangelists. They carried on the itinerant work modeled by Fraser.

The prayer movement led to a discipling and church-planting movement that sent out missionaries to neighboring countries. After forty years, the movement had grown to the point that half of the Yunnan Lisu were Christians. More than one-half of the seven hundred thousand or so Lisu in China today call themselves Christians, as do 75 to 90 percent of the Lisu in Myanmar and many of those in Thailand.[29]

29. McConnell, "Mission to the Lisu," 30.

3

Movement Leaders and Catalysts

Rapid multiplication is desirable in that many enter the kingdom of God in a short period of time. But leader maturation takes time and character is chiseled gradually. When discipleship does not produce enough mature leaders, the movement will struggle, falter, or become shallow. When new leaders are neglected, churches suffer, and future progress is curtailed. Sustainable, healthy growth requires a balanced attention to the making, maturation, and multiplication of disciples and leaders.

At the turn of the twentieth century, Gustav Warneck observed that where local leaders had taken over self-government rapidly as in Hawaii, Madagascar, and British Guiana, it "has erected a sham building destitute of solid foundations; everywhere inward and outward retrogression has been the consequence."[1] Leadership development is a critical part of gospel movements. Missionary control stifled movement, but indigenous leadership without adequate preparation also failed. The path forward is a balanced and synergistic relationship between making new disciples and growing existing ones.

If we do not want to reproduce *just any kind of church*, we will not want *just any kind of leader* but will intentionally invest in the character and skill development of emerging leaders. This should be self-evident. The development of disciples who become healthy leaders is the biggest contributor to healthy movements. Transformation and multiplication go hand in hand.

---

1. Warneck, *History of Missions*, 403.

What do healthy, missional leaders look like? They will have the character qualities required of church leaders in the New Testament and balance three salient values in their lives and ministries: The *Great Calling* to worship and glorify God in thought, word and action, the *Great Commandment* to love God and neighbor, and the *Great Commission* to make disciples according to Christ's teaching. These three dimensions, *Great Calling*, *Great Commandment*, and *Great Commission*, shine in churches when they are first and foremost woven into the lives of disciples and leaders.

MOVEMENT LEADERS

"Developing healthy, missional leaders is perhaps the most important key to healthy movements that are also growing movements."[2] Movement leaders are missional—they adopt the posture, thinking, behaviors, and practices of someone on mission with the gospel message—and that passion for mission flows from their relationship with God.

As indigenous local leaders do the work of the ministry, the Holy Spirit works through them to ignite and grow movements. They are gospel messengers, uniquely gifted and called by God to passionately spread the gospel, develop disciples, and establish new churches. The cultural insider, propelled by love, is God's delivery system. "He sums up in himself, in its most intense form, the longings of the times and interprets to his day and generation. He is not the creator of the movement but it's best interpreter."[3] The movement grows as God's local messengers make disciples and gather them in healthy biblical fellowships with recognized spiritual shepherds.

Characteristics of Movement Leaders

Emanuel Prinz has done the most comprehensive research to this date on the qualities of movement leaders. He identified eleven qualities found in all the leaders interviewed.

2. Ott, "Movement Maturity," 2.

3. Burns, *Revival*, 3.

Table 3.1

Traits of Effective Movement Leaders[4]

Hunger for God	They hunger for depth with God; yearn to love him more deeply; they seek to hear God's voice and be obedient.
Expectant Faith	They expect that God will grow a movement among their people group and save many soon, and they have great faith that God will show his power through their lives.
Confidence	They feel confident in their spiritual gifts and skills and exhibit a sense of confidence.
Drive for Responsibility	They feel responsible for the people they serve and for engaging them with the good news; they are motivated by a sense of responsibility.
Dependability	They are reliable and trustworthy; others can depend on them.
Persistence	They are tenacious despite challenges and amid difficulties; they don't give up.
Empowering	They empower and enable local people to be the key players by putting responsibility and authority in their hands from the beginning and by developing their gifts.
Confidence in the Holy Spirit	They are confident in the Holy Spirit and have faith in him to accomplish his intended work in the life of all God's children, as they are enabled to obey his commands.
Confidence in the Bible	They have deep confidence in the Bible to be their CPM guidebook, and deep assurance in its power to accomplish what God desires.
Influencing Beliefs	They talk about their most important values and beliefs, consider the moral consequences of decisions with people, and emphasize the importance of living toward the purpose for which one is created.
Inspiring of vision	They articulate a compelling vision of the future, talk enthusiastically about what needs to be accomplished to see a growing movement, and express confidence that goals will be achieved.

Although the leaders studied all attempted to use reproductive CPM approaches, they did not attribute their fruitfulness to the methods used. Prinz concludes that the person is more important than the strategy employed.[5]

4. Prinz, "Person, Not Method," para. 1.

5. Prinz, "Person, Not Method," para. 6.

Types of Movement Leaders

Leaders move forward and bring others in their wake, but they do not all have the same gifting or capacity. Movements also have different *types* of leaders. We can only offer an overview of the internal leadership of gospel movements. Nathan Shank, a strategy coordinator in South Asia known for developing the *four-fields model* of church planting, identified five levels of leaders in developed CPMs. Addison, working with Shank, describes of these *levels of movement leadership*:

- Level One: Seed sowers who engage lost people with the gospel.

- Level Two: Church planters who engage new fields, sow the Word, nurture the growth, and birth new churches.

- Level Three: Church-planting multipliers who successfully multiply new generations of church planters and churches.

- Level Four: Movement trainers who introduce biblical training for multiplying churches to pre-existing autonomous networks of churches.

- Level Five: Strategy coordinators who train and release leaders and mobilize networks to saturate a specific population segment.[6]

According to Shank, all disciples should be trained as level-one seed sowers and can be part of a church-planting team led by a level-two leader. Level-three leaders (church-planting multipliers) are the primary engine of the movement because they multiply workers in the harvest; but they need level-four (trainers) and level-five (strategy coordinators) leaders to equip them and come alongside them in the task. According to Shank, in a mature CPM, all five levels are needed, but level three to five leaders are in shorter supply.

The five levels do not represent an automatic leadership pathway from one level to another, although some will increase their capacity and sphere of activity as they grow. "Leaders need to find their personal levels of giftedness and calling. There is no hierarchy of value between levels of leadership. As we will see, a leader can only progress to the next level by becoming a servant who empowers others."[7]

6. Shank and Shank, "Four Fields," 108–15.

7. Addison, *Pioneering Movements*, 105.

MOVEMENT CATALYSTS

Here's our simple definition: *A movement catalyst is someone who comes alongside leaders to develop them and help them multiply healthy disciples, leaders, and churches.* They come alongside in a facilitative role. They are not the decision-makers but developers. As such they have a dual focus. They help leaders grow personally *and* become increasingly effective and fruitful in ministry. They share a common objective with the leaders: Together they invest selectively and strategically in the growth and reproduction of disciples, leaders, and churches.

Some students of movements believe that, for indigenous multiplication to occur, no external influence should be allowed. Spontaneous movements, without missionary presence, occur—but only rarely. Nathan Shank, who has worked with over fifty CPMs, made this observation in an interview by Steve Smith: "I've never seen a CPM—my definition would be multiple streams of fourth generation—that didn't have a parachuted Level Four initially as a catalyst."[8] In other words, external (parachuted) catalysts are usually needed initially, until local catalysts are in place. Here's why.

The gospel must travel from one culture to another to penetrate UPGs, and God has called his people to be the carriers. In pioneer settings, missionaries are needed to establish the first churches and develop its leaders. But they are transitional leaders who pass the baton to local leaders and shift to a facilitative role. Until the movement reaches a certain level of maturity, it will need external catalysts to develop and support local indigenous leaders. Later the primary catalysts will come from the local culture—internal catalysts. The need for them remains and grows as the movement reaches the missionary-sending phase.

Synergistic Partnership

The need for external catalysts is most obvious in the pioneer stage but continues to a lesser degree and in more focused ways as the movement takes shape. There is a synergetic effect when catalysts work together with local movement leaders. Catalysts are church-planting facilitators, rather than hands-on planters. They "serve as activators who provide a pathway and empowerment for emerging leaders toward multiplication ministries."[9] They develop local leaders and help them shepherd the movement.

8. Shank, "Multiplying Movement Pioneers."
9. Wilson, "Church-Planting Catalysts," 272.

Scaffolding comes in many shapes and sizes. In some places, construction workers walk precariously on thin logs tied together with strings. In others, steel is used to hold up sturdy planks. But, regardless, we can be sure of one thing: scaffolding was never designed to hold up the building. Catalysts are like scaffolding. They support the building while local leaders, the future pillars of the churches, are being established. They use a different style leadership from the start—facilitative leadership. They do not take over. Rather than control or direct what happens, they offer critical elements such as ideas, research, resources, teaching, skill-development, and encouragement.

The impact of external catalysts on gospel movements will only be as great as their success in developing, empowering, and strengthening cultural insiders. Amazing things happen when these two types of leaders, movement leaders and catalysts, work together. This is the vision behind this book: Mobilizing and equipping catalysts to come alongside movement leaders and create partnership for gospel movement throughout the world.

New Testament Examples

The idea of catalytic ministry, coming alongside local leaders, is not at all new, although the term may be unfamiliar. The Apostle Paul's ministry was shaped by the opportunities before him and the season of his life and ministry. He began as a pioneer church planter but transitioned to a facilitative role, as he turned responsibility over to local leaders. He became a global catalyst for the cause of Christ but retained the heart of a pioneer evangelist. He returned to churches his team had planted and corresponded with their leaders. Toward the end of his life, under house arrest, he preached the gospel (Acts 28:23–30) and continued to strengthen and defend the fledgling churches between Jerusalem and Rome by sending emissaries and epistles. He developed workers like Timothy, Titus, and Tychicus and coordinated their efforts (2 Tim 4:9–22).

Barnabas might well be the best biblical example of a catalyst. He served as a facilitator and bridge-person in the *Way*. He has been seen as a prototype for Christian coaching and mentoring, but those one-on-one ministries do not capture the full orb of his catalytic gospel ministry. He used his financial resources to provide for believers on pilgrimage in Jerusalem, mentored Saul, and gave John Mark a second chance. As an envoy sent to assess the situation in Syrian Antioch, he went beyond the call of duty, encouraging and strengthening the young church.

Some, like Paul and Barnabas, began as pioneer church planters but later prioritized a regional facilitative ministry. Paul spent most of his later years strengthening the churches, although he planned to continue pioneer work in Spain where the gospel had not been preached (Rom 15:20, 23–28). Timothy and Titus might also be called precursors to today's catalysts. They were never pioneer planters, as far as we can tell. Paul recruited them as assistants on his missionary teams. Later sent them as emissaries to strengthen young churches. They intervened to encourage and help local elders complete or correct some specific aspect of the work.

Examples in Missions History

We see this distinction between external catalysts (church-planting facilitators) and internal movement leaders in mission history as well. Many of the early pioneer missionaries, like those working among the Lisu (chap. 3), were restricted in their access to the people they wanted to reach and learned to use local evangelists as assistants or surrogates.

Waskom Pickett was sent to India to investigate mass movements among the outcastes and make recommendations, since voices in high places were questioning the validity of these group conversions. The mission to the Chuhra in the Punjab, begun in August 1855, led to a *people movement to Christ* (PMC). Missionaries baptized two converts on October 25, 1857. They kept these new believers on a missionary base for their protection. However, when a third Chuhra man, named Ditt, became a believer, he returned to his village to witness to his people. Despite the persecution he experienced, he led his wife, daughter, and two neighbors to the Lord and brought them to the missionaries to be baptized. After three months, Ditt returned with four other men. In ten years, over five hundred Chuhras were allowed into the church and after forty years the entire district was converted with few exceptions.[10]

Ditt's story highlights the untapped potential of local disciples who become disciple-makers, and the need to unleash the power of lay cultural insiders. The role of the missionary, though facilitative, was crucial. Ditt relied on them to help with teaching, baptism, and the selection and sending of evangelists.

A Lutheran work among the Chota Nagpur of East India provides another example. Initial contacts were made in 1845, and within five years, nineteen Western missionaries went out. Six died, and the rest were ill or

---

10. Pickett, *Christian Mass Movements*, 43–44.

discouraged—but they prayed and persevered. In the summer of 1850, four tribesmen visited the missionaries, claiming they wanted to see Jesus.

After trusting Christ, and receiving instruction, they were baptized and sent out to witness to their own people. By 1857, the church had grown to nine hundred baptized disciples and two thousand unbaptized inquirers. This rate of growth continued until Pickett wrote his book some eighty years later. Pickett identifies four common features to the PMCs he studied in India.[11]

- Missionaries and ministers did not seek to start these movements.
- They began with disciples who refused to be separated from their groups of origin.
- The real founder was not the missionary but the indigenous convert who went to his tribe with the gospel.
- The missionaries (external catalyst role) no longer viewed castes as obstacles but as channels for the spread of the gospel.[12]

We have argued that the ministry of a catalyst is not new. However, in this Facilitator Era, we are rediscovering and refining the catalyst role with greater intentionality. The gospel movement in the case study that follows is not yet a full-fledged CPM; but, in a region traditionally considered resistant to the gospel, churches reproduced to the fourth generation in twenty years, from 1997 to 2017. Whereas some movements have neglected the intentional development of disciples and missional leaders, this movement has made it a core commitment. Two friends in distinct ministries, Witwer and Sittser, are its primary catalysts.

AN EMERGING NORTH AMERICAN GOSPEL MOVEMENT

Greater Spokane, in eastern Washington, is nestled between the high desert of central Washington to the west, the Rockies to the north, and Idaho to the east. "Spokane" means "children of the sun" in the native Salish language. About six hundred thousand residents live in the greater Spokane metropolitan area, the sunny side of Washington State. Despite its distinct topography and climate, greater Spokane shares one feature of the Pacific Northwest (PNW). "Church-going is not a habit here," says Jerry Sittser,

---

11. Pickett, *Christian Mass Movements*, 45.

12. Pickett, *Christian Mass Movements*, 56.

professor of theology at Spokane's Whitworth University. Secularism is advancing more rapidly here than in most regions of the country. There are churches on many street corners, but they are largely empty on Sunday. Some sociologists believe that the PNW has become a breeding ground for countercultural expressions of faith largely because it never had a Christian culture.

A group of church leaders is stepping into this vacuum, considering this region a fertile field for church planting. They envision planting four hundred new churches in ten years by equipping church-planting interns to multiply churches. This ambitious goal would double the number of evangelical churches in this region and add as many as 120,000 witnesses, enough to change the spiritual landscape of the region.

Four friends who share a passion to see the gospel transform Spokane have formed an umbrella network.[13] Each one of them has taken on the challenge of recruiting five to seven incubator churches, churches that create an environment and provide resources to prepare, send out, and support church planters while they launch new churches. They will each take on a new church-planting intern every other year. Thus, there are four networks of incubator churches, each led by one of the four friends. Those churches also pledge to assist financially, find potential church planters, and give them practical experiences that will complement their conceptual training.

Sittser is designing a two-year program that will provide the educational piece. Participants can receive credit from Whitworth for their studies and learning activities. Through Sittser's advocacy, the university has received a financial grant from the Lilly Endowment's *Thriving in Ministry Initiative* to leverage the educational dimension of this church-planter development. The equipping model will provide support and development for the four network leaders, the pastors of incubator churches, and the interns. It will include:

- quarterly training events for the incubator churches, their leaders, and their church planter interns;

- monthly training events for the interns, following a twenty-four-month training cycle;

- network gatherings for planning and prayer led by the four network leaders, Richie, Mike, Joe, and Rob.

---

13. Those leaders of Spokane churches are Joe Wittwer (Life Center), Mike Meade (North Church), Richie Shaw (Real Life North), and Rob Fairbanks (Immanuel Spokane).

Life Center—an Umbrella Church

Pastor Joe Wittwer of Life Center exemplifies the passion for church multiplication shared by the partners of the umbrella group.[14] Faith Center in
Eugene, Oregon, sent him out to revitalize a struggling church in Spokane.
Faith Center also helped to start, or restart, seventy-five churches. Wittwer's
sister and brother-in-law started another church and went on to lead the
church-planting efforts of the Foursquare denomination.

Early on, Wittwer realized that the world would not be reached solely
by sending off church members to form a daughter church. Churches that
send off a group of members to start a new church, without actively making disciples, take a long time to bounce back, and sometimes never fully
recover. For movement to take place, daughter churches also need a culture
of reproduction and leaders passionate about reaching and discipling their
world for Christ. When Wittwer arrived in Spokane in 1978, those who did
not share his vision for church multiplication left the church. Only forty
people stayed—but they shared his church-planting vision.

In the years that followed, the church developed processes to make
disciples and disciple-makers that remain to this day. They ground new believers in the faith through a ten-week small group experience which helps
them find and follow Jesus. Through this intensive, these new Christians
learn to grow personally, relationally, and spiritually in a kingdom community. The church offers this discipling journey three times a year. The next
step is service. Following their ten-week journey, leaders encourage growing disciples to join a mission group serving locally or internationally. This
discipleship program feeds leadership growth and church reproduction.

Finally, in 1997, the mother church was ready to reproduce. Wittwer
describes the experience: "In 1997, we launched our first church plant: Summit Ridge on the South Hill. On our first Sunday, 635 people showed up
for worship! That's a big baby!"[15] About four hundred Life Center members
went over to help launch Summit. The attendance at Life Center was down
by forty—not four hundred; and it took a week—not two years—to fill the
empty seats.

Two years later, Life Center sent out another two hundred members
with a pastoral couple they had apprenticed, Mike and Tesa Meade, to form
Life Center North. On the first Sunday, 565 people showed up. That next
Sunday, the attendance of Life Center wasn't down two hundred; it was

---

14. For illustrative purposes, we are focusing on the story of the Life Center churches, but all four partners of the Spokane network have their own amazing stories to tell.

15. Wittwer, "Planting More Churches," section 2A.

up two hundred. Life Center North has in turn started several daughter churches and one granddaughter.

Then in 2002–2003, Life Center Church had twins! In September 2002, they launched LifeRoads at a public school in northeast Spokane, with 375 people at their first service. Four months later, they sent out their fourth church plant, Eastpoint. Since then, Life Center has planted or sponsored seven other churches, totaling eleven daughter churches, eleven granddaughters, two great-granddaughters, and two sponsored churches (table 3.2).[16]

Table 3.2
Life Center Church Planting History

Life Center Church—four generations of reproduction from 1997 to 2018[17]	
1932	*Spokane Foursquare Church*
Generation (Gen.) 1, 1978	Spokane Foursquare becomes *Life Center*
Gen. 2, 1997	*Summit Ridge* in Spokane's South Hill
Gen. 3, 2000	Summit Ridge planted *Living Hope*
Gen. 4, 2011	Living Hope church plant
Gen. 3, 2017	*Summit U*, a Gonzaga University satellite of Summit Ridge
Gen. 2, 1999	*North Church* in North Spokane
Gen. 3, 2001	*Foursquare Church* in Post Falls, ID
Gen. 3, 2006	*Church without Walls*, a house church model
Gen. 3, 2014	*The Heights* in Airway Heights, WA
Gen. 4, 2019	*Church Plant* from The Heights
Gen. 3, 2014	*Hillyard Life* in Spokane's Hillyard District
* Gen. 3, 2015	*Friendship Church* for special needs adults and families
Gen. 3, 2016	*Addy Foursquare* in Addy, WA
Gen. 2, 2002	*LifeRoads* in NE Spokane
Gen. 2, 2003	*Eastpoint* in Spokane Valley, WA
Gen. 3, 2013	*Uplift* planted by Eastpoint in Spokane Valley
Gen. 3, 2018	*Followers* planted by Eastpoint
Gen. 2, 2009	*City Church* in Spokane's Garland District.
Gen. 2, 2009	*West Central* in Spokane's West Central District
** Gen. 2, 2010	*Mosaic Fellowship Spokane* (interdenominational church)
Gen. 3, 2011	*The Seaside* planted in a bar by Mosaic

16. Five other daughter church plants have not survived for one reason or another.

17. Life Center (first generation) reproduced to the fourth generation.

**	Gen. 2, 2014	*Immanuel Spokane* (a Baptist church)
	Gen. 2, 2014	*Life Center CDA* in Coeur d'Alene, ID
	Gen. 2, 2015	*River City* in central Spokane
*	Gen. 2, 2015	*Life Center Kaliningrad*, Russia with US immigrant pastor
*	Gen. 2, 2019	*Life Center Slavic Church*
	Gen. 2, 2019	*Cheney Church* in Cheney, WA
* shows a cross-cultural church plant ** shows a sponsored church rather than a daughter		

Gospel Movement Characteristics

Why Spokane? Why now? Both Sittser and Wittwer affirm that this gospel movement is emerging at this time and place because God has brought together unique leaders with a shared vision. What do these men and women have in common?

Passion for Saturation Evangelism

According to Sittser, churches are greying and dying all around and 83 percent of the people remain unchurched. He is convinced God wants to start hundreds of new churches to reach them. One of the church planters started a church in an elementary school. He dreams of a church within walking distance of every resident and believes it could be done by renting space in local schools throughout the city. Sittser calls this a *new parish model.*

The goal is God-sized. They are working toward doubling the number of churches in ten years. When talking to these men, you sense excitement and determination. Seeds sown and watered in prayer are bearing fruit. The four umbrella churches are all seeing new churches started. Momentum is growing.

A Multiplication DNA

"The best situation is when recently planted churches build church planting into their DNA so that every church assumes it will plant a church," affirms Sittser. Other churches in Spokane have planted daughters occasionally, without infusing in them the vision and responsibility to do the same. This creates occasional addition, not multiplication. Wittwer's corrective is to organize the church as a *disciple factory* that regularly sends people out to launch new churches. New churches are the overflow of the discipleship ministry. He expressed the vision of multiplication this way to Life Center members:

> Johnny Appleseed wanted everyone in America to enjoy apples. But he didn't go across America passing out apples! He planted apple trees. We want to win the world for Jesus. We can't just pass out apples, we have to plant apple trees. We can't just win a few people to Jesus; we have to plant churches that will win people to Jesus, who will plant more churches to win more people to Jesus.[18]

Focus on Developing People

Programs don't plant churches—people do. To plant four hundred new churches in Spokane, it will take many more church-planting leaders. The four umbrella churches have each recruited about twenty other churches that will host interns. The chart below shows the potential of new churches coming from the two-year apprenticeship training (table 3.2).

Table 3.2
Potential Church Multiplication by Apprenticing Church Planters

Year 1	Year 2	Year 3	Year 4	. . . Year 10
20 churches	30 churches	40 churches	60 churches	. . . 400 churches

However, multiplication that yields four hundred churches presupposes that successive generations of churches and pastors share the vision and determination of the network leaders. The strategic plan to apprentice planters and pastors could sustain that kind of multiplication—if the passion of the founders is transmitted to others without getting bogged down in logistics or derailed by conflict.

18. Wittwer, introduction to "Planting More Churches."

Collaboration Rooted in Relationships

The catalysts who joined hands to transform greater Spokane have history together. Their dream of church multiplication in the PNW had been brewing for a while. A decade earlier, Sittser and Wittwer mentored a cohort of fifteen young church planters together over a period of five years. These apprentices learned from each other and prayed together. They read early Christian sources and discussed the application of their reading to life and ministry. Most of the participants in that monthly cohort have joined the church-planting network, so that the early mentoring effort laid a foundation for what is happening now.

These kingdom workers have different doctrines and opinions, but they chose not to let those things stand in the way. Sittser helps to hold them together as advisor, equipper, and catalyst. Since the churches vary in size and giving capacity, each contributes a yearly amount to the cause. They are still figuring out what to hold in common and what should be at the discretion of the local church.

Vision toward the Future

Gospel movements are birthed by God and carried along by those he calls and leads. The DNA is set when disciples and churches reproduce over several generations. This movement began when two friends joined hands to mentor a young crop of students with a passion to transform their city. These two original catalysts recruited two others and the four churches they lead have already started dozens of daughter and granddaughter churches. Their gospel witness is transforming thousands of lives. Yet they are still in the formation stage of the gospel movement. When asked what the greatest contributor to the movement launch was, Wittwer responded without hesitation: "Leaders who share a vision to disciple their city."

Catalysts cast the vision and set the DNA. Wittwer and Sittser were not satisfied to launch a large multi-venue church or even a new cluster of churches, as noble as those achievements would be. They envisioned a movement that would transform the spiritual landscape of Greater Spokane and work toward it through concerted prayer, consistent disciple making, and kingdom collaboration; and they infected others with that vision. What does the future hold? Sittser believes God could use this movement as a model for other regions: "It would be nice if others would ask 'what is happening here?'"

Why a gospel movement? That is the question we take up next.

4

Why Gospel Movements?

There is a vision behind each gospel movement. Wittwer and Sittser dreamed of something big—a work of God that would bring many to Christ and transform their region. They prayed and God answered, leading them to include others. They gathered a cohort of students and are now leading a church-planting battalion.

Some start planting a church because they want to create something new—a uniquely relevant or impactful church, or a specific type of congregation. There's nothing wrong with that. But movement leaders and catalysts want to see entire people groups, cities, and countries revolutionized by the gospel. Not everyone will launch a gospel movement, however there are many good reasons to be part of one.

THE IMPACT OF GOSPEL MOVEMENTS

Gospel Movements Bring Glory to God

Gospel movements reach more people because they saturate entire regions with gospel light. Jesus said that disciples glorify his father when they bear much fruit (John 15). God's glory should be the primary reason for attempting great things. When people accomplish the safe and expected—the things within their reach—they can attribute the results to human effort or strategy. But gospel movements defy human explanation; they point to God's timing, power, and grace. Gospel movements are his doing, and they fulfill his promise (Matt 24:14). They remind us that Jesus is building his church and that the gates of hell will not prevail (Matt 16:18). They challenge us to persevere until Jesus has worshippers among every people group.

Gospel Movements Produce Abundant Harvests

Wherever the gospel took root in Acts, churches reproduced and traveled across ethnic and geographic boundaries to make Christ known. Gospel movements are needed to reach the nations. This pattern should be the expectation, not the exception. The norm should never be a sterile church without daughters and granddaughters; or a church that remains ethnocentric, indifferent to the unreached around her.

Besides, we will never win the world through addition because occasional church planting does not keep up with the birth rate. Disciple and church multiplication, in the hands of everyday disciples filled with the Holy Spirit, was God's original design and remains the only way to keep up with population growth and complete Jesus' mandate.

As of this writing, Long has documented 1,369 movements around the world, and believes there are more. Those movements represent over 1 percent of the world's population, at least 77 million disciples in 4.8 million churches. In addition, there are 4,500 current efforts to engage unreached peoples with a movement approach around the world.[1]

Gospel Movements Can Penetrate Any Environment

Some believe that it takes an explosive CPM to reach a people group. However, a closer look shows that gospel movements of modest but steady growth can also usher great numbers into the kingdom. Many of these movements are unspectacular, but collectively powerful in influence. As *evangélicos* in Latin America have openly and joyfully shared their faith in Jesus, they have given rise to gospel movements of many shapes and sizes.

According to church growth studies, the number of Evangelical believers in Latin America tripled in the twenty-five years between 1985 and 2010, and the percentage of Christians grew at twice the rate of population growth.[2] Yet, CPMs have been noticeably absent, except for one that occurred in Cuba

1. Long, "One Percent," 38.

2. Mandryk, *Operation World*, 46–47.

in the 1990s. Indeed, in Nicaragua, Brazil, El Salvador, Jamaica, Guatemala, and Puerto Rico the twenty-year church growth exceeded that of Cuba, the one Latin American country that experienced a CPM.[3]

For example, the percentage of Evangelicals in Nicaragua has flourished from 6.3 percent to almost 30 percent in twenty-five years and averaged an annual growth rate of 5.5 percent.[4] Over the same period the percentage of Evangelicals in Cuba went from 2.1 percent to 8.8 percent as can be seen in table 4.1.[5] Cuba's church growth was over 10 percent for the decade when the CPM exploded (1990–2000) but leveled off after that. That story follows.

Table 4.1

Contrast between Church Growth in Cuba (CPM) and Nicaragua

Country	2010 population in millions	Annual population growth rate	Percent of Evangelicals in 1985	Percent of Evangelicals in 2010	Evangelical average annual growth rate
Cuba	11.2	0.02%	2.1%	8.8%	3.5%
Nicaragua	5.8	1.31%	6.3%	29.8%	5.5%

Long helps to put the current impact of CPMs in perspective. It would be a mistake to focus *exclusively* on existing CPM strategies that come from rural contexts.

> While they remain a small percentage of the world, they are not insignificant. Disciples in movements make up 1% of our world's population, and many movements have emerged in some of the most spiritually hungry regions . . . Within the next five to ten years, we could easily see the current 1% become 2% of the world, and almost certainly significantly more within specific areas of focus.[6]

Our world population is becoming increasing urban, segmented, and individualistic. While large people movements to Christ are needed and expected to have a growing impact, our cities and post-Christian, secular societies call for coalitions of gospel movement initiatives for their diverse populations.

3. This can be seen by comparing *Operation World* percentages of Evangelical believers from 1990 to 2010.

4. Mandryk, *Operation World*, 634–35.

5. Mandryk, *Operation World*, 291–92.

6. Long, "One Percent," 42.

Gospel Movements Span Generations

Some churches launch as many churches as possible in one generation, without regard to succeeding ones. Like a human mother, they soon reach their reproductive capacity. However, movement-minded churches see the greater potential of generational growth and invest their energy and resources in successive waves of planting. Through indirect influence, they extend their impact until Christ returns. Diet Schindler illustrates the power of generational reproduction:

> My wife's grandparents had been married for more than seventy-five years when they died. Grandpa was 105 and Grandma 97 years old, and they left behind progeny of over 150. In their lifetime, they saw themselves forwarded into five generations! Imagine holding a fifth-generation baby in your arms, knowing you and your spouse were the first cause! . . . Great church planting counts the generations, not just the number of children it has fostered.[7]

Movement-minded leaders like Wittwer and Sittser invest in people and efforts that span the generations. Their primary focus is not on a particular method or ministry, but on finding and developing reproducers.

Gospel Movements Bring Lasting Transformation

Transformation is the outward manifestation of the gospel's inner working. It is the very nature of the gospel to bring deep life change. The history of missions overflows with examples of positive change. William Carey and his partners established schools and medical work in India and pioneered social reforms including banning the *sati* burning of widows at the funerals of their deceased husbands. Mary Slessor, a Scottish Presbyterian missionary to Nigeria, is still famous in that country for the humanitarian changes she brought, most notably for having stopped the common practice of infanticide of twins among the Ibibio people.

In China, lotus feet, small feet with high arches shaped by binding, were considered a status symbol as well as a mark of beauty. The practice of foot binding began as an attempt to refine the feet of young dancers among the elite and gradually spread to most classes. However, the process was extremely painful and often resulted in lifelong disabilities. Christians discouraged the barbaric practice and helped bring an end to it.

---

7. Schindler, "Church Planting Multiplication," 2.

Missionaries can set the example, but ultimately local believers must provide the impetus for transformation. For decades in Japan, Christianity has been a foreigner's religion. Only a fraction of one percent would consider themselves practicing Christians.[8] However, a quiet and gradual change is taking place in Tohoku, on the northern coast, where a tsunami hit with devastating force in 2011, tragically killing close to twenty thousand people, causing three hundred billion US dollars of damage, and reconfiguring the coastline for years to come.

Devastation brought the fast-paced Japanese to a screeching stop and jolted their perspective on life. Christians who previously had an isolationist mindset, became gripped with compassion, and joined thousands of expatriate Christians from around the world in relief efforts. Christians shared the love of Jesus in the hope that, as the region rebuilds, Christianity will be an integral part of the fabric of society. There is a new openness to Christians. "In the northern part of Japan, where the earthquake and tsunami hit, the church now has a stronger presence in society," says scholar Atsuyoshi Fujiwara in an interview for *Christianity Today*.[9] New churches have taken root, and local people see Christians in a new light.

Gospel Movements Improve the Social Fabric of Communities

Of course, not all gospel movements have been equally able, or willing, to challenge unjust laws and evil practices. But where they have, they have become a force for good among the oppressed and downtrodden. The gospel, lived out authentically in the Spirit's power, improves the condition of people on the margins of society. Of course, change takes time and impacts one community at a time, as seen by the following account.

Jesús Pérez was a successful businessman, who owned two businesses in the Dominican Republic. As he began thinking of retirement, he remembered a beautiful property in the mountainous village where his brother lived. The place was called Los Agachaos—the hunched over ones. This was an apt description, because the town was known for family feuding, drunkenness, and gambling, resulting in much brokenness. And Jesús's brother was one of the broken ones—a town drunk. Los Agachaos was without electricity, schools, sewer systems, paved roads, or phones. Nevertheless, it was set in a beautiful part of the countryside, and Jesús bought land and built a home overlooking the valley.

---

8 Mandryk, *Operation World*, 489.

9. Morgan, "Fresh Encounter," 45.

It saddened him to see the hardship and deprivation; and he decided to do what he could to help the villagers. First, he asked the city leaders if they would be interested in having a church in the community. The answer was a firm, "No, Señor." So, he decided to start in his home and invited the town leaders to have their official meetings there. They agreed. Then he asked if they could begin their meetings with prayer. Since they believed in God, it certainly wouldn't hurt to have his blessing. A few months later, he asked if they could read a portion of Scripture. Would it do any harm to honor him by reading his Word?

After a while, Jesús's brother came to faith in Christ. His life was marvelously transformed. People started taking notice and the two brothers had many opportunities to share about Jesus' transforming power. The town leaders started to see real improvements in the community as well. Over time, the village changed. Roads were paved, and electricity was brought in from Jarabacoa. As a result, the village added more stores and a school. The city leaders decided to close the liquor store.

Then Jesús invited those who wanted to thank God to meet in his home for worship services on Sunday. Some accepted, including town leaders. The town was becoming a pleasant place in which to live, so Jesús suggested they change its name from Los Agachaos to Buenos Aires—Good Winds. Jesús offered them a parcel of land on which to build a church building so more people could worship God. This time they accepted.

This story shows the impact a person can make in a village. But what does it take to change the social landscape of a region, city, or country? Instead of asserting that an individual acting alone can change her world (not very believable) or saying that one church can change society (rarely seen), Timothy Keller wisely suggests that many churches and ministries working together can bring about a sustained and profound change to culture.[10]

A critical mass of engaged Christians can shift the balance and produce systemic change. It takes many new churches and life-giving ministries that flow from them. God raises up salt and light disciples through gospel movements. When socially engaged disciples multiply, and churches permeate the city, their combined impact reaches a tipping point. Then the gospel spreads and churches form a new moral ecosystem, an environment where healthy transformation can flourish and produce lasting change.

10. Keller, *Center Church*, 366–77.

Gospel Movements Survive Persecution

God's gracious work through movements does not stand unopposed. The enemy tried to divide, derail, and destroy the early church. Yet God prevailed, and it grew. The church that launched the first gospel movement suffered terribly throughout the following decades.

Persecution broke out immediately (Acts 8) and persisted after a time of peace (9:31). According to F. F. Bruce, the murder of James, Jesus' brother, and the destruction of Jerusalem, along with its economic and social structures, were devastating blows to the Judean church. "When, according to Epiphanius, Hadrian paid a visit to the site early in his reign, he found there seven poor synagogues and one small church."[11] Eventually, the believers dispersed, and the center of Jewish Christianity shifted from Jerusalem to Damascus and other Middle Eastern cities. Yet the Christian movement survived and became international.

Deep, sustained opposition can make or break a movement. The church in North Africa, which flourished in the age of Augustine and Tertullian, was decimated largely because it was not part of an indigenous movement. "There are two main reasons for the disappearance of the church. First the Bible was never translated into the language of the people . . . Therefore, secondly Christianity never penetrated the native culture to any great depth."[12] When churches are part of an indigenous gospel movement, they are more likely to survive than when they stand alone. This has been true of the persecuted church in China, Ethiopia, and Cuba. The following account is a story of God giving birth to an indigenous movement under an oppressive regime.

A GOSPEL MOVEMENT IN CUBA

The name *Los Pinos Nuevos*, the young pines, reflects the homegrown nature of this gospel movement. José Martí, a hero of Cuba's independence from Spain, used the expression in a famous speech referring to Cuba's need for new leaders. Apparently, while visiting Tampa, Florida, he saw a vicious fire destroy a pine forest. He later realized that from those charred remains, a new forest of green pines would emerge and gave a famous speech that popularized the expression.

The movement *Los Pinos Nuevos* (LPN) started modestly in the 1920s when a Cuban and a North American came together with a dream of developing gospel workers for the region. In 1928, well before the Cuban

11. Bruce, *New Testament History*, 389.

12. Steele, *Not in Vain*, 5.

Revolution, a Cuban who wanted pastoral training in Spanish, and could afford it, would have to study in San Jose, Costa Rica. Few could manage that, and those who went did not always return. Pastor Bartolomé Lavastida and missionary Elmer Thompson teamed up to address this need by developing a local Bible school in Santa Clara, Cuba. Their vision was to see a gospel church led by biblically sound and fully committed servants in every town and village of Cuba.

Lavastida had a dramatic conversion which fueled his passion to reach his people. Revolutionaries killed his father while he had been studying in the United States. He returned to seek revenge. Instead, he met a Christian who helped him find forgiveness in Christ. In time, he became a pastor and promoter of leadership development.

During the global economic crisis of 1929, the school started without outside financial backing. Lavastida claimed at a meeting that he had a school board that would never let him down. A skeptic asked, "And who is on that board?" Lavastida replied, "The Father, the Son, and the Holy Spirit. They will never abandon me."[13] The values of these two founders remain central to the movement: A life of prayer and surrender, constant gospel sowing, and vibrant faith in God.

Lavastida's vision to make disciples throughout the island was adopted by the LPN association that emerged from their ministry. Initially the students were all Presbyterian, but soon they were coming from the Baptists, Methodists, other denominations, and independent churches. In May 1935, the school was officially registered with the government. It flourished and was respected by all Evangelicals. Thompson developed the school while Lavastida oversaw the churches planted by its graduates.[14]

The leaders launched a printing operation and produced evangelistic literature and a monthly publication called *Misionero Bíblico* (Biblical Missionary). To get the gospel message into every home, they established a radio station that broadcast for twenty years until the Cuban Revolution. Lavastida also helped Thompson form the *West Indies Mission* to send Cubans and other Bible school graduates as missionaries. As a result, new works were started in Haiti, Africa, and the Canary Islands.

LPN leaders developed a doctrinal position based on the Word of God, without importing outside formulations. They decided that graduates of the school should start the churches to preserve the biblical worldview and ethos of the movement. In 1941, they registered with the government

---

13. Amelia, "Iglesia Los Pinos Nuevos (Falcón)."

14. Amelia, "Iglesia Los Pinos Nuevos (Falcón)."

as a Cuban Evangelical Association and have remained faithful to the Word and to their founding principles.[15]

The movement, launched with great faith and vision, came upon hard times during the Cuban Revolution. Initially, many Christians supported the uprising and rejoiced over the end of the corrupt Batista regime. But then the Castro government clamped down on the churches and imposed unwarranted restrictions to control the different facets of society.

The decade of the 1960s was especially hard. The government strictly prohibited ministry outside religious buildings and regular hours of service. Private schools were closed, and the ministry of education indoctrinated children from Christian families with atheistic materialism in nationalized public schools. Some pastors suffered jail sentences of several years. Missionaries were expelled or left voluntarily.

Thus, Evangelical churches operated largely in survival mode, with little church planting and limited contact with the outside world between 1960 and 1990. They tended to be orthodox but also traditional, emphasizing separation from the world rather than transforming the world through the gospel. Ministry was centered in local church buildings, where Christians met several days a week. The pastor led the church and lay leaders assisted, but did not preach, teach, or lead services. Then a crisis shook things up.

> Against Cuba's wishes, in September 1991, Soviet troops began withdrawing from Cuba . . . By December 21, 1991, the Soviet Union had imploded, leaving its global partners without its military or economic support. The Cold War had ended, and Cuba found herself alone and isolated, without political friends or military allies.[16]

Cuba, abandoned by her major patron, experienced shortages of food and clothing that made life difficult for most households. The economy tanked, food was rationed, and people suffered severe deprivations. With those changes came a crisis of security and hope. Yet, communist indoctrination had not done away with the underlying belief in God, and people flocked to the churches until the church buildings could no longer accommodate the growth.

A group of Protestant pastors went to the chief of the Office of Religious Affairs to ask that they be allowed to reopen boarded-up church buildings and build new ones. The Communist party official denied their

---

15. Registered churches in Cuba have a legal standing and limited freedoms. They are closely monitored and need to seek permission to have speakers from outside Cuba or for activities beyond their normal services.

16. Urbanek, *Cuba's Great Awakening*, 89.

request but suggested an unexpected alternative. He recommended that they meet in homes: "Why don't you hold meetings in your houses like the Pentecostals? Near to where I live is one of these houses, and they hardly let us get any sleep. But for now, we cannot authorize the construction of any new buildings."[17]

The Cuban pastors took this official at his word and *casa cultos* (house churches) were started as satellites of the existing churches to accommodate the influx. Up to this point, the traditional way of starting a church was to find a Bible school graduate and pair him with a lay leader from the mother church. Together, they would begin a *mission* in the community where the new church was planned. The work was not recognized until it had a pastor, a Sunday School, and ministries that were expected of all churches. Then they would apply for a permit to secure a meeting place. This could take years. But, because of the sudden influx of people, churches began to develop lay pastors and *casas culto*.

Initially, they saw these changes as a temporary measure dictated by necessity; but, in time, house churches became enduring Christian communities. Denominational leaders recognized that these spiritual families gathered, developed, and cared for many who would not enter an official church building. Because of the shortage of trained pastors, they trained lay leaders on-the-job and deployed them to meet the need.

Traditional church fellowships continued, but alongside them, *casas cultos* spread throughout the country, saturating the cities, and creating a need for different types of training strategies. The LPN Bible school, which had a four-year undergraduate program to prepare pastors and missionaries, broadened its reach by adding a decentralized program to prepare bi-vocational workers through evening classes. This decentralization of ministry equipped and empowered of a fresh wave of Christian workers to meet the growing need for teaching and spiritual care.

The LPN movement grew exponentially as did the Baptist, Methodist, and Pentecostal churches. LPN leaders reported 51,114 baptisms in the two-year period between the end of 2014 and 2016.[18] These numbers were later confirmed by Jonatan Hernandez Roche, Cuban missionary, and LPN statistician. According to Kurt Urbanek's doctoral study, Baptist congregations went from 238 to 7,039 churches in the twenty years from 1990 to 2010. The Assemblies of God (AOG) soared from eighty-nine churches in 1990 to 10,776 by 2010. That number grew to almost 50,000 by 2015.[19]

---

17. Urbanek, *Cuba's Great Awakening*, 98.

18. Austvold, "Superintendent Ministry Report," 1.

19. Urbanek, *Cuba's Great Awakening*, 116–30.

Omar Rodriguez, ReachGlobal's international leader for Latin America and the Caribbean, reported that in 2015, the LPN training program had 44,277 students in 359 training centers, touching some twenty-three different denominations and 49,983 house groups. He added:

> God is doing something that goes beyond anything that I have ever experienced. And it's not just the numbers, these people live from a fountain of hardship that has been used by God to mold a body that is as clear and focused regarding the Gospel as I can possibly imagine. Grace, mercy, justice flow in a way that makes the power of God evident in people's lives.[20]

Pastor Bartolomé Lavastida and missionary Elmer Thompson served as the initial catalysts of LPN, a vast network composed of clusters of churches surrounded by house fellowships. Despite its rural roots, the movement is making Cuba's cities a priority. It has established a significant presence in the capital, La Havana, and in most provincial capitals. Their vision is a movement that founds biblical, contextualized, reproducing churches, centered in the gospel of Christ, that in turn impact the different spheres of Cuban society. With that in mind, they have developed the 10-10-5-10 plan: ten regional CPMs, in ten major cities, in five years, with ten farms to help to sustain the ministry.

Gospel movements experience growth spurts and plateaus. Since the pope's visit in September 2015, there has been an easing of tensions. How will the relaxation of Communist control impact the movement? It is too early to say, but some trends are emerging.

Three years after the pontiff's visit, Rodriguez described the school and movement as gaining maturity and continuing its mission, although the numbers have leveled off. "The denomination has a clear vision and mature leadership. They are planning on sending out missionaries . . . Churches continue to be planted and most churches are vibrant."[21]

Other groups that experienced rapid growth are also plateauing. The number of AOG churches and house groups declined from 2015 (49,903) to 2018 (27,830).[22] The numerical decline is most likely due to the emigration of church leaders and a grouping of house churches to form larger assemblies.

LPN faces some significant challenges and dangers. Church leaders and members have left for the sake of their families. With increased exposure and travel, some Cuban church leaders are tempted to adopt imported

20. Rodriguez, "Ministry Report," 1.
21. Rodriguez, "Ministry Report," 1.
22. Urbanek, *Cuba's Great Awakening*, 111–30.

Western forms from North America that are not locally sustainable. They need wisdom and restraint to preserve the indigenous values and multiplication DNA gained during the hard times.

The picture of new pines appearing from the scarred remains of a forest fire raises the question of movement emergence. For a movement to appear, there must be a spark of life and a source that sustains that vital energy. This is true of all living things. Steve Addison summarizes the spiritual dynamics behind movements:

> God takes the initiative. God chooses unlikely people, far from the center of ecclesiastical power, and He works to remake them inside out. He inspires innovative insights regarding His mission, and how it is to be carried out. Biblical truths and practices are rediscovered. A growing band of ordinary people emerges who have heartfelt faith and missionary zeal that knows no bounds . . . Movements change people, and changed people change the world.[23]

Gospel movements are spiritual at their core—and everything that is spiritual requires spiritual means from the start. But how is spiritual vitality discerned and nurtured? In the pages that follow we look at six *primary leading indicators of spiritual vitality* that contribute to movement emergence and growth.

---

23. Addison, *Movements*, 22, 29.

5

Emergence Factors

God is the author of gospel movements. Like the wind, we can observe signs of his activity although we never see the divine actor himself (John 3:6–8). The Spirit sends out gospel witnesses, convicts the world of sin, opens the eyes of unbelievers, changes lives, nurtures faith, and motivates service— and *he does this through his people, the church.* Rick Warren reminds us, "The church is the most brilliant concept ever created. It has outlasted cultures, governments, skeptics, and enemies from within and without, and it will continue to do so until Christ returns."[1]

But the churches are dead apart from the work of the Spirit. Spirit-filled Christians, bring spiritual momentum that propels gospel movements. Spiritual renewal and revival have historically given rise to new missionary advances. Then the gospel travels outward in power, crossing frontiers and surmounting obstacles. Overcoming spiritual opposition, the Word advances and the church grows, just as Jesus said it would (Matt 16:18).

> Church planting remains fundamentally a spiritual enterprise that requires spiritual means found only in the Holy Spirit. And all the human effort, strategy, talent, resources, and creative genius that go into church planting are vain unless endowed with his life-giving power. This is not only a pervasive pattern in Acts but a theological principle: No church planter will be successful apart from the agency, leading, and filling of the Holy Spirit.[2]

1. Preface to Ott and Wilson, *Global Church Planting*, vii.
2. Ott and Wilson, *Global Church Planting*, 46–47.

If this is true, we want to know what kinetic (producing movement or energizing) forces are involved? God is unlimited in his means. We offer no formula, but confidently affirm that *the same dynamic forces at play in the New Testament gospel movements are transforming the world today*. Thus, we look to the works of the Holy Spirit in Acts to guide us to leading indicators.

LEADING INDICATORS OF SPIRITUAL VITALITY IN THE NEW TESTAMENT AND TODAY

Gospel movements are remarkable in their diversity, yet they have similar spiritual dynamics. Power, boldness, and joy of the Spirit, absent prior to Pentecost, became characteristic of the apostles afterward. Every obstacle became an occasion for fervent and sustained prayer and an opportunity to see God intervene. Disciples accepted sacrifice and suffering for Jesus. The six spiritual dynamics that follow (table 5.1) stand out in every phase of gospel expansion and in all the diverse movements we will describe. While they do not comprise an exhaustive list, they represent some salient qualities of dynamic gospel movements in Acts and in the world today. Simply put, no gospel movement will rise above its level of spiritual vitality evidenced by these qualities.

Table 5.1
Six leading indicators of spiritual vitality

Prayerful dependence	*Spirit empowerment*	*Willingness to sacrifice and suffer*
Abundant gospel sowing	*Biblical integrity*	*Kingdom-minded cooperation*

Prayerful Dependence

Gospel movements are born in prayer and advance through prayer. In Acts, intercession is the *umbilical fluid* from which the church was born (1:14), a central practice of the local fellowships (2:42, 12:5), and a priority that the apostles protected (6:4). The disciples' corporate prayer is fervent, consistent, and often spontaneous. Likewise, throughout history, prayer has preceded and saturated missionary progress. The gospel takes root in new regions as the Holy Spirit musters his church to pray, send, and evangelize.

As evidenced in the life and ministry of J. O. Fraser, prayer is *the tip of the spear* in the effort to launch gospel movements. Spiritual battles for

UPGs must be won in prayer before the gospel can penetrate on the ground. Those who hope to advance gospel movements apart from fervent, sustained prayer underestimate Satan's grip on the unsaved. Friendships can create opportunities and compassion ministry can bring favor, but without prayer, they are powerless to change hearts and minds.

John D. Robb, former chairman for the International Prayer Council, and director of prayer ministries for World Vision, documents many cases where prayer led to a spiritual breakthrough, particularly when the Iron curtain fell.

> In the dramatic events of the last year in Eastern Europe God has used the prayers of His people to shake the nations. He can do the same thing in the unevangelized world. He is seeking those who will stand before him in the gap for the 2,000 major unreached peoples . . . Prayer is at its very heart a linking activity. First, prayer links us with God to receive His power and direction as we pray for the world and carry out our own ministries. Secondly, as we pray for the unevangelized world, it links us with unreached groups and the Christian workers laboring among them. It links our efforts and their efforts to God in His almightiness, without whose help all such efforts ultimately are in vain.[3]

Abundant Gospel Sowing

For the gospel to be good news, it must spread. Evangelism, more than a duty or discipline, is a hallmark of gospel movements. Sharing Christ with others is not only a responsibility of all believers but also a natural expression of their love for him. Spirit-filled believers want all to know Jesus and honor him as Lord of all.

> Spirit-empowered [gospel] proclamation plays a pivotal role in the book of Acts, and it is the very source from which church planting flows . . . This is the methodological foundation on which the churches described in Acts were built, and it is the model we are to follow today.[4]

Through passionate evangelism, Nagaland, in northeast India, became the state with the highest percentage of Baptists in the world. This state of two million, squeezed between Assam and Myanmar, was successively controlled by Burma and Great Britain. In 1963, it became a self-governing

3. Robb, "Prayer as a Strategic Weapon," 2, 4.
4. Ott and Wilson, *Global Church Planting*, 47.

state within India. But the most surprising fact is that over 90 percent of its people claim to be Christians, and the great majority of them—75 percent—Baptists. How did this come about?

The Naga people were animists who worshiped spirits. They sought to appease the evil ones and curry the favor of the powerful ones. They were also headhunters who collected skulls as trophies (but not cannibals). It was partially because of these savage practices that the British would later encourage missionaries to work among them. Missionaries working in neighboring Assam reached the first two Nagas in 1847. They were taken in and taught but died before they could take the gospel to their people.[5]

Twenty-two years later, American Baptist missionaries Edwin and Mary Clark began work among the Naga. The people had a deep sense of sin and believed in a highly personal God, associated with the sky, that stood above all others as the God who sustains everything.[6] The Naga listened to the message, but they also weighed the consequences of following Christ's teaching. Their whole way of life would have to change. Eventually, some could not resist the truth about Jesus.

The Clarks could not enter Nagaland, so they sent in an evangelist from Assam. That man returned with nine new disciples. They were baptized and founded the first Naga church on the border. It took several decades for the gospel to take root and spread. Mary Clark started the first schools in Nagaland, one for boys and one for girls. The following graph describes the remarkable growth of the Naga Church in seventy years between 1890 and 1960 (table 5.2).

Table 5.2
Church Growth in Nagaland from 1890 to 1960[7]

Decade	Net growth	Rate of Growth	Naga Preachers
1890–1900	307	409 %	12
1900–1910	246	195 %	90
1910–1920	3,697	328 %	100
1920–1930	12,749	264 %	250
1930–1940	18,738	107 %	250
1940–1950	41,233	114 %	145
1950–1960	4,173	5 %	140

5. Moses, "Baptists of Nagaland," para. 23.

6. Richardson, *Eternity in their Hearts*, 90.

7. Moses, "Edwin Clark," para. 17.

What an amazing gospel movement! There were never over ten foreign missionaries in Nagaland, and most served in education, social work, and medical ministries. They were catalysts supporting the work of the Naga evangelists and pastors. The Clarks left in 1910, but the gospel spread through Naga evangelists who went out in successive waves to unreached tribes and villages. By the 1950s, most Nagas had heard the gospel and had accepted or firmly rejected it. This could explain the slower rate of growth in that decade. Today Naga missionaries take the gospel that transformed them to other places.

Spirit Empowerment

Before Jesus ascended to his father, he taught his disciples to abide in him and pray in his name. After telling them to make disciples, he told them to stay and wait for the outpouring of the Holy Spirit (Acts 1:4–5). The first servants in the church were "known to be full of the Holy Spirit" (Acts 6:3). Empowering by the Holy Spirit is an absolute necessity and a primary qualification for all service. God makes spiritual gifts and spiritual power for ministry available to all his people (Eph 4; Rom 12; 1 Cor 12). The Holy Spirit remains constant, but his infilling is not residual, and his enabling should never be taken for granted (Rom 8:5–11). "As Supreme Administrator of the church and Chief Strategist of the missionary enterprise . . . it is abundantly evident in the record that the Holy Spirit is jealous of His prerogatives and will not delegate His power or authority to secular or carnal hands."[8]

There is a direct correspondence between this Spirit-given missional impulse and church planting. The church in Nepal grew at a rate close to 11 percent per year (somewhat faster than in China) from 1970 to 2013.[9] In 1952, there was only one known fellowship of believers in the country, the Ramghat Church of Pokhara.[10] It all started with a small mission group called Nepal Evangelistic Band. By 2015, there were over ten thousand churches. This growth occurred during forty years of totalitarian Hindu monarchy, followed by a protracted civil war. After a decade of relative freedom, the Nepalese church is once again facing restrictions and threats, yet it continues to evangelize. The churches want to reach the 103 people groups in their country. To do so, they depend on God and work together in his mission.

8. Sanders, *Spiritual Leadership*, 98.

9. Johnson, *Christianity in Global Context*, 38.

10. Das, "Christianity in Nepal," para. 28.

A man who attended our basic church-planter training said, "The Holy Spirit is making living water spring out from the ground, but you are giving us funnels to make it go further." Krishna had been making disciples but thought he could not plant churches because he had no formal pastoral education. After our training, he received permission from his pastor to plant new churches according to the biblical pathway he had learned. Between 2012 and 2018, he started sixteen new fellowships in resistant Hindu settings. He aspires to start fifty new churches in unchurched towns and villages. He also reproduced the training by taking teams with him on evangelistic excursions to villages in the Himalayas. Several of those he apprenticed have started churches. Together they are on track to exceed the fifty new churches. He radiates the love and joy of the Holy Spirit.

Biblical Integrity

Spiritual vitality and biblical integrity are twin engines of gospel movements. By biblical integrity, we mean faithfulness to biblical truth as the bedrock and living guide of the movement, shaping its every dimension.

A high view of Scripture was a trademark of the New Testament authors and of Jesus himself. The apostles appealed to them and based their preaching on them. They spoke with confidence as they quoted the Scriptures in their messages. Six times in Acts, we encounter an expression like, "but the Word of God continued to spread and increase" (Acts 12:24). The Word of the Lord is personified as a living agent advancing Christ's kingdom. It is living and powerful calling people to repentance and faith and transforming the lives that respond.

Today as well, gospel movements draw their authority from the Word. Though faithfulness to the Word alone does not guarantee that a movement will thrive, it is necessary for true discipleship and church growth. Most emerging gospel movements are Christocentric and put more stock in biblical essentials than in theological formulations.

Jesus says, "Therefore everyone who hears these words of mine and puts them into practice is like a wise man who builds his house on the rock" (7:24). His Great Commission includes, "teaching them *to observe* all that I have commanded you." We are not talking about sterile Bible knowledge. Submission and obedience are essential. Transformation comes from truth applied to life. People often emphasize either spiritual vitality or biblical integrity. However, healthy movements thrive when they serve as twin buttresses, and stagnated movements need to recover both to experience a fresh wave of growth.

Willingness to Sacrifice and Suffer

Paul writes, "I will stay on in Ephesus until Pentecost, because a great door for effective work has opened to me, *and there are many who oppose me*" (1 Cor 16:9). He did not see spiritual opposition as a closed door. Persecution came as a reaction to the profound transformation taking place in Ephesus. Demetrius led an uprising that threatened their very lives. Salvation is free, but discipleship is costly.

In Acts 4, the authorities commanded the early church not to speak of Jesus (the first anti-conversion law) and threatened reprisals should they continue. Jesus' followers did not pray for their safety but asked for boldness to stand firm and continue proclaiming his name. After their impromptu prayer meeting, they were filled with the Spirit and continued to share the message courageously.

Gospel movements do not flourish because of favorable circumstances and freedom of speech. They thrive when Christians risk favor and freedom to make Christ known. Where the church has the luxury of liberty and affluence, followers of Jesus can easily become comfortable and complacent. But when evangelism is illegal, they must make a choice: Comply and avoid reprisals or witness and risk ostracism and outright persecution.

The worst part of the Cultural Revolution in China lasted from 1966 to 1976. Revolutionary guards violently persecuted Christians. The church went underground but was not silenced. It is still growing at an average annual rate of 10 percent. That means that the church in China doubles in size every ten years—despite the lack of freedoms. What the Chinese underground churches lack in rights and resources, they more than make up for in commitment and sacrificial service. They see opposition as part of the normal Christian life.

Kingdom-Minded Cooperation

The Apostle Paul included men and women from diverse backgrounds on his missionary teams. In Romans 16, he shows his high regard for his co-workers by calling them "tested and approved in Christ," "hard workers," and "chosen in the Lord." Paul pleads with two of them "to agree together in the Lord" and to work together (Phil 2:2). Such was the value he placed on unity in Christ's service.

Social movements typically emphasize their unique beliefs and practices. However, in gospel movements, Christians emphasize what they hold in common and work together on that basis. The gospel transcends their differences as they cooperate around a common vision for their city, country, or region. Of course, cooperation with every group is not possible, but catalysts learn to foster a spirit of collaboration and rally people from different ecclesial backgrounds in the cause of Christ.

These six leading indicators of spiritual vitality are interacting manifestations of the indwelling life and power of Jesus. He motivates fervent prayer, loving witness, trusting dependence, courage in suffering, obedience to the Word, and joyful collaboration for the kingdom's sake. There are other generative forces at play in gospel movements, but unless these ones are present and growing in the lives of the disciples and leaders, the churches will flounder and fail to reproduce.

SPIRITUAL RENEWAL IN BRAZIL

This is a turn-around story about a church that sparked a small movement in a time of crisis. In 2018, the Convenção de las Igrejas Evangélicas Livres (Convention of Evangelical Free Churches of Brazil or CIELB) movement of churches celebrated its fifty-eighth birthday. God used many people to take it from one church to an association of about fifty churches, spread throughout Brazil, with its own missionary-sending body. It is still a relatively small movement, but, considering its humble beginnings, a remarkable one none the less.

In 1960, the first missionaries of the Allianz Mission, the missionary-sending agency of the German Free Churches, arrived in Xanxerê, a city in the southern province of Santa Catarina, Brazil. Other missionaries settled near Brazil's frontier, along the jungle in western Paraná, and began a new church in Toledo. In both regions, the work grew slowly at first. On April 21, 1984, they founded the Convention of Free Evangelical Churches in Brazil with only seven churches spread out over several provinces.[11]

Pioneer Penetration in Santa Catarina Province

The work in Santa Catarina province began modestly when two families met together to study the Bible and pray in the town of Blumenau. After a careful search, they invited a German Free Church missionary to shepherd this growing group. He stayed for six years. When it was time for him and his family to return to Germany, the small fellowship chose a young Brazilian, recently graduated from Theological School, as its pastor. There were

---

11. "Nossa História," *AMEL*, http://amel.org.br/quem-somos/#historia.

only seventeen church members when Claudio Ebert began, but he had plenty of contacts in the local community, having worked with the local branch of Youth for Christ.

Claudio started discipling young people, growing the church, and forming home groups called *family groups*. He trained leaders for the church's ministries and family groups. The church emphasized evangelism and discipleship, and a couple times a year, the groups came together to baptize all those who had come to Christ.

Local Multiplication

Pastor Claudio sent out workers in 1987 to plant two new churches during his first year as pastor. Despite a lack of training and financial support, the Brazilian church planters showed amazing dedication to the task. In fourteen years, while starting five daughter churches, the Blumenau mother church grew to approximately a thousand members that met in a converted warehouse. They also formed dozens of family groups that met in carports and homes throughout the region. The church had many of the qualities of a large missional church: a charismatic and visionary senior pastor, a complementary pastoral team, an effective church-based training program, and a well-coordinated small group network with evangelistic and caring ministries. But they also had a vision to cover the province with new churches.

Regional Development and Organization

Starting in 1997, the German mission began turning the leadership of the movement over to the Brazilians and helped them establish a decentralized theological school for the equipping of pastors and missionaries called *Seminário Teológico nas Igrejas Evangélicas Livres* (SETIEL). They offered courses in the various regions to make equipping accessible to those already involved in ministry. The association chose three priorities for the twenty-first century: Christian Education (at all levels), Missions, and Church Planting. ReachGlobal missionary Mike Gunderson began praying for a church-planting movement and worked to organize a church-planting course as part of their SETIEL program. In 2002, my wife and I taught SETIEL's first church-planting course.

Seeds of Renewal

The pastors and missionaries who took part in the course were very respon-
sive, hungry for a way to start many new churches that did not require salaries and expensive buildings. They realized that the New Testament pattern
provided an alternative to the financially dependent, pastor-centric model
of church planting most common in Brazil and much of the Western world.
We discussed new paradigms of lay movement during five unforgettable
ten-hour days. When we talked about God's work through church-planting
movements, the question emerged, "Why are we not seeing this kind of
movement?" They humbly confessed that the reasons listed below were
holding them back (table 5.3):

Table 5.3

Obstacles to Multiplication according to Brazilian Leaders

Lack of missionary vision	Lack of financial and human resources
Excessive preoccupation with the estab-	Lack of motivation and leadership
lished church	No adequate church-planting strategy
Faulty theology or missiology—reflec-	Lack of training for church planting
tion and teaching	The church doesn't beat with the heart
Not disposed, not willing to pay the	of God
price	Sin and spiritual coldness
Lack of conviction or of call	
Inability to work on a team or	
independence	
Satan doesn't want it	

This led to a time of confession and calling on God. Afterward, one for
them declared, "Today is the first day of a new church-planting movement
in Brazil." The final day, after the teaching was over, a few of the leaders
drafted a resolution. The entire group signed it, pledging to do everything in
their power to multiply disciples, leaders, and churches. Later, the association of churches adopted the same pledge at their annual convention and
chose a national church-planting catalyst, Johny Stutzer, to lead their efforts.
In the years that followed, under Johny's leadership, the CIELB contextualized training, mobilized workers, and sped up church planting.

Regrettably, Claudio Ebert, one of the main church-planting leaders,
resigned suddenly. This created uncertainty and leadership tension. Yet
the vision for church planting continued, and many were faithful to their
church-planting covenant. The Blumenau mother church released some
of the family groups to form new local churches, which in turn planted

daughter churches. Thus, the paradigm went from a megachurch with family groups to a networked cluster of reproducing churches.

The Blumenau mother church also launched a church plant, led by Johny Stutzer, in a neighboring province, Rio do Sul. That church has started three daughter churches. The association launched pioneer work in five other regions, so that now there are churches spread throughout the country in nine provinces.

Global Participation

The church in Toledo, Paraná, situated at the edge of the Amazon and exposed to indigenous groups, has been a leader in missions. They have sent missionaries to the Amapá and Kulina peoples. Their passion to reach the unevangelized helped the CIELB start its own sending organization called AMEL (Associação Missionária Evangélica Livre or Evangelical Free Missionary Association) which works in partnership with the Free Evangelical Church of Germany. Together they have sent missionaries to Madagascar, Portuguese-speaking Mozambique, Portugal, and Haiti.

The national board recognized the need for support systems to strengthen church planting. The multiplication vision and training came initially from missionary catalysts like Mike Gunderson. But Brazilians soon took the lead. From 2007 to 2010, Johny Stutzer's team developed training for church planters and formed a national church-planting network. In December 2010, Johny and his team offered a Church Planting Bootcamp in Blumenau to forty-five lay leaders, pastors and missionaries interested church planting through organic reproduction. Many recommitted themselves to multiply churches. In 2007 seventeen new CIELB churches were at some stage of development, many of these in Santa Catarina province.

The CIELB gospel movement, after three decades of growth, recognizes its need for revitalization. The vision for church planting remains strong, but it will not go far unless renewal leads to fresh waves of discipleship. One hopeful sign is that a new generation of leaders is emerging.

Jesus told his disciples, "The Holy Spirit will give you power, and you will be my witnesses." God's power is given to serve his purposes. No gospel movement, no church, no Christian can rise above its level of spiritual life, prayer, and Great Commission engagement. The six indicators of spiritual vitality found in gospel movements do not exist in a vacuum. Gospel movements draw their vitality and growth from their connection to Jesus, the True Vine. All ministry must flow from him. So, when that first love and passion wanes, leaders and catalysts of gospel movements must help the people return to the source.

Movements are never static. Churches and associations of churches, like people, go through stages of growth and decline. A fellowship of churches is either moving closer to what God intended or it is drifting away. When they grow as God intended, they move through stages of movement maturity culminating in new movements. Understanding this movement maturation process helps leaders assess growth and determine what is needed to move forward.

6

Movement Maturation Process

Gospel movements, like all living things, go through stages of growth. They are born, develop, and eventually decline.[1] At any given point, they are either growing or regressing, unable to remain stagnant for long. This idea of a movement life process should not surprise us. Ever since the Adamic fall, all living things on earth have a beginning and an end—a birth date and an expiration date. This is also true of ministries, local churches, and groups of churches. How many of today's denominations were around when Luther nailed his theses on the door of the Wittenberg Castle church? Thank God the gospel does not have an expiration date. It brings growth, renewal, and new birth to Christian movements.

GOSPEL MOVEMENTS FOLLOW A LIFE PROCESS

Steve Addison describes the typical journey of movements through the birth, growth, maturity, decline, and decay.[2] These growth stages are like seasons of life. After generations of growth, fueled by first love, movements often battle institutionalism or complacency. Decline can come from external factors, but also from within. False doctrine, division, or worldliness steal momentum and undermine spiritual vitality. The journey from birth

---

1. This leveling off is documented in the Baptist movement of Nagaland and in *Los Pinos Nuevos* in Cuba. The story of the CIEB in Brazil illustrates how a spiritual awakening can turn a dormant movement around.

2. Addison, *Rise and Fall of Movements*, 1759.

to decay is the pattern expected of movements in a fallen world, but not the norm for gospel movements led by Spirit-filled servants.

We find movement maturation in the New Testament as well. Paul laid a foundation by starting churches, but he did not stop there. He cared that those churches grow in love, unity, and truth, and that they reproduce. He wanted them to glorify God, honor Christ, and become mature, "attaining to the whole measure of the fullness of Christ" (Eph 4:13). He invited them to contribute to his mission by providing workers and resources for future stages of expansion.

Maturing movements gave birth to new infant ones as the gospel moved from culture to culture until, by the end of the first century AD. it had spread east to Spain and along the North African coast, reaching the Roman province of Africa.[3] Today, healthy movements, characterized by the six leading indicators of spiritual vitality (chap. 5), stay the course for generations and launch other movements by sending out missionaries to the unreached. The journey from birth to decay is not an inescapable sentence or a uniform progression. Because Christ overcame death and Satan and lives in the church, movements can turn around. The gospel movement started in Corinth, though plagued by moral and spiritual attacks, recovered, and eventually sent missionaries to help Paul in his work.

> Rebirth can occur at any point in Maturity and Decline. The earlier the intervention, the greater the chances of success. Movements are not reborn through human creativity or design. Rebirth is more than improvement; it is a journey from death to life and is only achieved by returning to the Word, the Spirit, and the Mission. It is a work of God.[4]

Addison underlines the only path to movement revitalization—a return to life through God's Spirit, under his Word, focused on his mission. The missionary movements in Acts typically moved through four progressive levels of movement maturity before giving birth to new movements as seen in table 6.1.

---

3. Bruce, *New Testament History*, 415.

4. Addison, *Rise and Fall of Movements*, 17.

STAGES OF MOVEMENT MATURITY

Table 6.1

Stages of Movement Maturity

First Stage: Pioneer Penetration	Second Stage: Local Multiplication	Third Stage: Regional Organization	Fourth Stage: Global Participation
Main Goal: Planting the first indigenous churches in a contextual and reproducible way.	*Main Goal:* Establishing a sustainable pattern of church planting and reproduction by locals.	*Main Goal:* Forming a synergistic association/network of churches with a missional vision.	*Main Goal:* Sending out local believers on cross-cultural mission so that the movement reproduces.
Catalytic Role: Develop the first disciples and leaders and pass the baton.	*Catalytic Role:* Assist, coach, and partner with locals as they multiply churches.	*Catalytic Role:* Counsel and train movement leaders (formal and nonformal development).	*Catalytic Role:* Advise and support the deployment of missionaries and help with infrastructure.
Strategic Key: DNA of healthy, sustainable reproduction.	*Strategic Key:* Reproducible models that truly multiply and sustain health.	*Strategic Key:* Healthy biblical leaders and organic structures that reproduce.	*Strategic Key:* Partnership with good relationships and complementary contributions to a common vision.
Dangers: Non-reproducible methods, non-contextualization, discouragement.	*Dangers:* Stagnation, unhealthy dependency, weak leadership.	*Dangers:* Institutionalism, imposed structures, excess, or top-heavy organization.	*Dangers:* Zeal without wisdom, inadequate support structures, unstable finances.

The stages in the life process of a gospel movements are not automatic. They are optimal rather than absolute. We outline the growth pattern of a healthy movement that leads to new pioneer work, recognizing that these stages are not wooden. Even spiritually healthy movements experience plateaus and setbacks, but they get back on track. The movement that came from Ephesus will serve as a case study throughout our description of the four stages.

Stage One: Pioneer Penetration

Pioneer Penetration begins with the initial efforts to share the gospel, make disciples, and gather new believers in fellowships. Apostolic (missionary) teams get the work started. Peter traveled throughout Judea founding communities of believers (Acts 9:32). Philip laid a foundation in Samaria (Acts 8), and Paul and his teams established beachheads throughout much of the Mediterranean world, along the axis of Jerusalem to Spain. The goal was always to see the first disciples and churches take root in culturally appropriate and locally sustainable ways, so they could reproduce and have a transforming gospel impact. What is mission-critical in this stage?

> The shape of the first churches planted typically becomes the model for those that follow. Thus, establishing a missional-ecclesial DNA that is easily reproduced will be a key to long-term growth, reproduction, and health. This often requires employing methods that initially are slower but have greater potential for long-term multiplication . . . Attention must also be given to contextualize churches that are able to adequately communicate and live out the gospel in culturally relevant ways.[5]

Methods and means should be shaped by the context. There is a *coming of age* when leaders, churches, and ministries are locally developed, stable, and reproducing. The quality and reproductive pattern of disciple making is critical in this stage.

Ephesus Movement in the Pioneer Penetration Stage

Paul initially preached in the local synagogue in Ephesus, then left Aquila and Priscilla to do the discipling groundwork with Apollos and others (Acts 18:24–26). He later rejoined the team and resumed his proclamation in the synagogue (Acts 19:1–9).[6] When the synagogue leaders hardened to the gospel, the apostolic team moved to the School of Tyrannus and continued making disciples there.

Paul comments about this stage: "A great door for effective work has opened to me and there are many who oppose me" (1 Cor 16:9). People were healed, and evil spirits cast out (Acts 19:12). All were seized with awe and held the name of the Lord Jesus Christ in high honor (19:17). Public

5. Ott, "Movement Maturity," 9.

6. F. F. Bruce (1977) thinks Apollos and the twelve disciples of John the Baptist may have come from that synagogue and have helped to launch the movement.

confession of sin and repentance from sorcery broke out (19:18–19). This led to a decline in the worship of Artemis and a riot against the young church (19:23–34). The gospel touched different strata of society, including provincial officials (19:31). In summary, in this stage the gospel penetrates, and the initial churches are planted, leading to new life and social transformation, with opposition as a natural outcome.

Stage Two: Local Multiplication

Local multiplication can be summarized by the words: evangelize, establish, equip, and expand, which represent ongoing stages in the discipling process toward multiplication (figure 6.2).

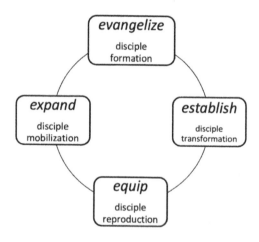

Figure 6.2. *Stages of discipling process toward multiplication*

Once a disciple-making pattern is established and the initial churches are started, local witnesses and evangelists move out and extend the CPM. This local expansion is carried on primarily by first-generation Christians from the local culture.

In Acts, this phase is often undocumented because the narrative focuses on the work of pioneers—Peter, Paul, and the apostolic teams. But, here and there, we capture glimpses of it. During Paul's second missionary journey, he only stayed three weeks in Thessalonica. Yet the reputation and witness of the Thessalonian disciples powerfully influenced the entire Greek peninsula. "The Lord's message rang out from you not only in Macedonia and Achaia—your faith in God has become known everywhere" (1 Thess

1:8). That *ringing out* or ripple effect speaks of local multiplication. What is mission-critical in the local multiplication stage?

> At least two conditions are critical at this phase. First, churches must develop in a healthy manner with spiritual vitality, sound theology, and spiritual leaders. Second, local believers must take the lead in facilitating churches planting churches with minimal dependence on outside resources . . . Local leadership, not only in pastoral care, but also in evangelism, discipleship, and church planting is essential to a self-reproducing movement.[7]

Sometimes, the pioneers who start the work remain as equippers, coaches, and partners. This is healthy provided they pass the ministry baton to local leaders and transition to a facilitative role. Unfortunately, some pioneers stay too long and unintentionally hinder the work of local multiplication. They continue to occupy the center stage, instead of working from the margins. Others use methods that are not reproducible or culturally appropriate, making a transition to local leadership awkward. But ideally, pioneers step back to empower and assist the local leaders. Thus, for multiplication to take place, there must be a movement vision and a culture of empowerment, not control. A plan and pathway to grow local leaders is needed for leadership growth to keep pace with new church starts.

Ephesus Movement in the Local Multiplication Stage

In the local multiplication stage, Paul, Apollos, Aquila, and Priscilla raised up a local team of workers based in the School of Tyrannus. Timothy and Erastus were also there for some time (Acts 19:22). After two years the entire Province of Asia had been exposed to the message (Acts 19:10). "In this way the word of the Lord spread widely and grew in power" (Acts 19:20).

Epaphras extended gospel ministry to neighboring Colossae, Laodicea, and, most likely, Hierapolis (Col 4:12–13). Tychicus, another associate of Paul, helped to form a cluster of churches in Asia Minor (2 Tim 4:12; 1 Cor 16:19). Others also started works in Smyrna, Pergamum, Thyatira, Sardis, and Philadelphia (Rev 2–3), cities along a circular commercial route in the Lycus Valley near Ephesus. Miletus and Troas (Acts 20:6–38) are probably daughter churches as well.

---

7. Ott, "Movement Maturity," 9.

Stage Three: Regional Organization

In the third phase, *Regional Organization*, the church-planting efforts are strengthened and structured by establishing people and processes that sustain growth. Paul returned to the places where he had been on his previous pioneering trips to deal with problems and strengthen the work. He sometimes sent his associates to follow up and wrote letters to the young churches to help them grow and deal with moral and doctrinal issues. Most Pauline epistles were penned during his missionary journeys while churches were still being established.

In this stage, obstacles must be faced and overcome. Regional collaboration becomes important. Timothy and Titus both worked in Corinth to correct problems and bring church unity. Timothy and Erastus followed up in Macedonia, where the church endured great persecution, while Paul remained in Ephesus (Acts 19:22). Titus went to Crete to complete what they left undone, the selection of trustworthy deacons and elders. The role Paul's associates played anticipates the ministry of catalysts in many ways (see chap. 8).

> As the number of churches increases, the need for cooperation and organization also increases. There are many needs that can be best met by churches working together on projects such as training workers . . . and creating a sense of fellowship and mutual commitment among the churches. Churches may need formal representation and the ability to speak with a common voice to the government . . . Shared conferences and publications can create a sense of unity among the churches. Charitable efforts and social projects can be coordinated for greater impact and efficiency.[8]

Although we resist organization for its own sake, we recognize that all living things have an internal structure that grows and evolves with time. The focus is on developing people and support structures to facilitate further growth. Churches that do not turn inward but form a healthy missional association (or network) will be poised to send missionaries beyond their borders in the next stage. Catalysts can help them improve the selection, training, coaching, and development of new church planters. These church-planting systems need to be malleable and developed in context, keeping complexity and cost to a minimum. We will return to this in chapter 10.

8. Ott, "Movement Maturity," 10.

Ephesus Movement in the Regional Organization Stage

What happened to this movement in later years? A movement can become mired down in the organizational stage, or it can become a launching pad for missions. Paul equipped and deployed workers to strengthen the movement in Asia Minor, helping it respond to opposition, and grow. He wrote half of his epistles to churches in this region, or to people associated with those churches. He returned three or four years after the riot in Ephesus, taught the elders, and conversed affectionately with them, remembering the past and warning of difficult times ahead. What was the result?

From the book of Revelation, we know a network of churches emerged—how many, we do not know. The seven listed in Revelation were not the only ones, not even the major ones. Troas, Cyzicus, Magnesia, and Tralleis were considered more important.[9] The churches in Asia Minor became important defenders of Christian truths in the face of heresy by hosting international church councils in the fourth and fifth centuries.

Stage Four: Global Participation

During the fourth and final phase, Global Participation, missionaries are sent out to unreached people groups. Unnamed men from Cyprus and Cyrene traveled north from Jerusalem and established the church in Syrian Antioch. That church sent out Paul and Barnabas, who planted churches in Corinth and Ephesus. Men and women in the mold of Epaphras and Erastus went out from Ephesus and Corinth to take the gospel even farther. Mature gospel movements are also missionary movements that spawn new gospel initiatives. James Edwin Orr has written extensively about revivals that lead to new pioneer missionary work. He traces cross-cultural penetrations of the gospel in India, Korea, and other countries back to awakenings in the United States, Wales, and England.[10]

This stage flows from the regional organization stage in which missionary-sending structures are created and workers developed. This was true of the Evangelical Free Church of America. Just before the nineteenth century, recently established movements of Swedish and Norwegian immigrant churches in the American Midwest formed an association to train pastors and send missionaries overseas. Decades later, the movement adopted a mission statement that reflects that early commitment: "We exist to glory God by multiplying transformational churches among all people."

9. Ramsay, *Saint Paul the Traveler*, 274.

10. See Orr, *Second Evangelical Awakening*.

Ephesus Movement in the Global Participation Stage

The Ephesian movement lost something along the way. In Revelation, the Apostle John describes a hard-working church, perseverant, devoted to orthodoxy, and faithful in everything external; but one that abandoned her first love—a church in need of repentance and revitalization. Jesus lovingly confronts her, "You have forsaken your first love. Remember the height from which you have fallen. Repent and do the things you did at first" (Rev 2:4–5).

The church in Ephesus survived, since Ignatius, writing a generation later, still spoke highly of her. She became a regional center of orthodoxy, the seat of bishops, from which the Nicene Creed was affirmed, and the Cypriot Church recognized. Eventually, economic decline, coastal erosion, which made the port useless, and invasion by the Turks brought an end to this beacon of light, however, not before it gave birth to a movement. The story of this influential church speaks of the need to keep one's own spiritual torch aflame, while planting churches.

RELEVANCE OF MOVEMENT MATURATION

Why is it important to recognize that movements go through stages? Movements, like people, have different needs according to the stage they are in. Evangelists and church planters help birth churches. Waterers or developers help them mature. Others are skilled at helping stagnant ones experience a new season of fruitfulness.

Understanding these stages may also avoid unnecessary conflict about what types of Christian workers are most strategic and worthy of support. Is it best to support residential pioneer missionaries, traveling equippers and facilitators, or just send resources directly to the local leaders? We often set these approaches against each other. According to Ott, the choice of whom to support should depend on the stage of movement maturity. "The role of missionaries should not be determined by a one size fits all strategy, but rather by understanding the developmental phases of church planting movements, and by wisely contributing to the further maturity of these movements and their involvement in global mission."[11]

These stages also provide a grid that helps catalysts determine how best to assist a gospel movement in another culture. When we describe these four stages of movement maturity to movement leaders in the Majority World, they have often been able to situate their movement on the scale.

11. Ott, "Movement Maturity," 1.

That allows us to discuss how to move forward toward greater maturity. Recently, in Myanmar, the leaders of the Miso church movement realized that they had rapidly, within six decades, moved through the four stages and sent out fifty missionaries. But they confessed that they had sent them out without training and invited our team of catalysts to partner with them in church planter and missionary preparation.

CATALYTIC MINISTRY ACCORDING TO
THE STAGES OF MOVEMENT MATURITY

Church-planting catalysts can make good use of these stages to assess movement maturity and adjust their ministry accordingly. In the *Pioneer Penetration* stage, they may help the church-planting team do research and develop an entry strategy to evangelize and disciple in contextually appropriate ways. Then they can add value by coaching and advising indigenous workers during the early years when they need help establishing the first churches.

During the *Local Multiplication* phase, catalysts assist local leaders in the process of setting a DNA of disciple making and church reproduction. Emerging leaders must be developed in a reproducible way, so they can apprentice others (2 Tim 2:2). A wise facilitator will help the local leadership team assess their effectiveness in discipleship and leadership development and make changes without taking over the driver's seat.

In the *Regional Organization* stage, catalysts can use their experience to help leaders develop structures that serve growth and reproduction, rather than standing in their way (see chap. 10). Often, they can rally leaders from different backgrounds around regional events and efforts. Some movements may need help deepening theological reflection. Although local leaders are the best contextualizing agents, catalysts from the outside can ask questions and provide an outside perspective.[12]

In the *Global Participation* stage, catalysts may facilitate research to select UPGs and identify cultural bridges to effective gospel communication. Financial resources should be used cautiously to avoid undermining multiplication or creating ministries that depend on outside funds. Trusted catalysts will help local churches send their own missionaries. Understanding these four stages also helps local leaders take the pulse of their church family and identify steps toward revitalization—if the vision has leaked or the growth has stalled.

12. Hiebert, *Anthropological Insights*, 191–96.

STAGES OF MOVEMENT MATURITY
IN LIBERIA, AFRICA

The growth from pioneer penetration to global participation occurred in only twenty years in a movement called the Evangelical Free Church of West Africa (EFCWA). Liberia was established, colonized, and controlled by citizens of the United States as a colony for former slaves and their free black descendants. It started as a Christian state in 1847, but Freemasonry, imported by the early settlers and linked to indigenous tribal secret societies, penetrated nearly every sphere of life and church. Later, corruption and war devastated the land and destroyed much of the economy for two decades. A civil war raged from 1989 to 1996 and from 1999 to 2003. An entire generation of young people received no schooling. In the wake of this social disruption, Saudi Arabia funded economic and educational projects, paving the road for Islam's advance. Muslims have gained a foothold in the north, especially among the Mandingo and Vai ethnic groups, and they are progressively moving south to the consternation of the churches.

Stage One: Pioneer Penetration

Amid this chaos and spiritual battle, David Kiamu, a young Liberian Bible college student, believed that he and his friends could equip young disciples to start and lead simple fellowships of believers. He invited another Bible college student and three high school students to form the team that founded the EFCWA. This small group officially launched the first church on January 14, 1996, in Congo Town, one of the poorer neighborhoods of Monrovia, the capital city of Liberia. The first service took place in an abandoned building in the fish market section, with an attendance of 104 people. David, though still a student, became the pastor, and James, the other Bible college student, served as his assistant.

A year later, in 1997, one of the founding members moved to another district and started a Bible study in her house. David joined them once a week for six months. That community grew to forty-eight people, and became the second church, Grace Evangelical Free Church (EFC). A third church joined the movement. Then Titus Davis, a student that David was mentoring, started a Bible study class that became the fourth church, Hope EFC. Then Fellowship EFC was started, and the expansion continued.

Three factors stand out in the pioneer penetration stage: the visionary leadership of the first leaders, the faith and spiritual vitality of the people, and their compassionate concern for the immediate and eternal welfare of those around them.

Visionary Leadership

God's heart for the lost was evident in those young EFCWA leaders. In April 2007, Kiamu took part in an all-night prayer vigil in which a trans-African group of leaders asked the Lord, "What part of the vision to reach 100 million people belongs to us here in Africa?" ReachAfrica, an African mission born out of that night of prayer, is a lasting fruit of that passion to fulfill the Great Commission wholeheartedly (see *The ReachAfrica Story* in chap. 9). These pioneers also exemplify sacrificial service. Davis supported his family and ministry by working as a schoolteacher. He is fond of saying, "It is our responsibility as Africans to reach Africa," as he models locally sustainable ministry. None of ReachAfrica's country leaders are salaried for their leadership role in the movement.

Spiritual Vitality of the People

Davis affirms, "God is the source of growth and victory. Disciples are made, and churches are planted by the Spirit of God. Transformation can only come from the gospel." God has blessed the sacrificial obedience of people who serve without expecting any salary or reward. They are engaged in a spiritual battle, and Satan will not release people under his reign without a fight. So, they mobilize prayer and fasting, and practice prayer walks. They developed a prayer team that uses cell phones and the Internet to share prayer needs quickly, and a prayer chain by which requests move back-and-forth between movement leaders, regional leaders, local pastors, and house church leaders.

Compassionate Concern

During the civil wars in Liberia and the Ivory Coast, Christians visited the sick and dying, cared for refugees, took in orphans, and brought aid to the poor and hungry. They reached out in creative ways to specific communities through holistic ministries and disaster relief. That love was a powerful testimony that helped the churches grow. In addition, micro-finance and agriculture projects contributed to economic development and ministry support.

Evangelism and discipling, coupled with acts of mercy, are changing the spiritual landscape of Monrovia. Community development initiatives like the *Jesus Film* and *Seed Projects* have led to new discipleship groups. Church members decided to improve education at every level and worked to provide access to primary education and college scholarships. Churches started schools, not for profit, but to ensure that neighborhood children have a good start in life.

By 2015, the Monrovia mother church operated a primary school with over two hundred children. Some students met in cramped classrooms divided by makeshift reed mats without electricity or running water. But most children met in open air "classrooms" under the shade of trees. The members built everything themselves with scant help from outsiders and nothing from the government. Teachers lack the most basic materials and receive barely enough compensation to purchase rice for the month. When asked how they survive, Davis replied, "We have to. Our children are the future of the country, and they must be educated, whatever it takes."

Stage Two: Local Multiplication

In ten years, the church that started in the fish market grew into a movement of sixteen congregations. Some met in homes, others in rented buildings. One was a mobile church that reached drug addicts in the marketplace. They reached out to former child soldiers who were emotionally damaged from the civil war. Their inexpensive private school was inundated with students.

Eventually, they purchased a twenty-acre parcel of land to produce food for needy families and dug a well to provide water for the farm and drinking water for a nearby village. With a vision to equip church plant-ers and missionaries, they built a training center for disciples, leaders, and workers on the farm. Then they gave the apprentice workers job training, so they could provide for their families while developing their ministry skills.

Davis and other EFCWA leaders have adapted the multiplication strategy of Disciple-Making Movements (DMM) to their situation. Streams of disciple making, and Discovery Bible Studies (DBS), reached four gen-erations and accounted for hundreds of new disciples! They invited those interested to join a DBS in a home, coffee shop, or on church property. Here is the pattern set by Eleazer, an EFCWA leader from the Ganta region.

- Generation 1: Eleazar discipled seven individuals.
- Generation 2: Those seven discipled 36 others.
- Generation 3: The 36 discipled 216 others.

- Generation 4: The 216 continue to disciple others.

After the fourth generation, the evolution became too hard to track, so they started a new stream. Eleazar trained others to do this using DBS. He had seven DMM trainings scheduled in July and August 2018. Discipleship training strengthens the churches and leads to the planting of new churches.

Stage Three: Regional Organization

EFCWA leaders are known for their spirit of cooperation in a context where denominations most often compete for members and money. In 2010, five distinct associations came together to strategize and equip church planters to reach Liberia's least evangelized regions. They agreed to used Church Multiplication Training (CMT) developed by David Kiamu in consultation with our team of catalysts. Then they formed a parity agreement through which each group took responsibility for a region of the country. This heightened cooperation and minimized competition. But unity did not come from a memorandum of understanding. They enjoyed serving Jesus together and did not let their differences come between them. Outsiders commented: "When we see these groups that don't normally get along working together, we think, 'This must be a work of God.'"

Leadership development was a challenge. Few of the EFCWA leaders had been to Bible college. Character and skills were largely honed through on-the-job apprenticeship, although modular training and workshops have played an important complementary role. The in-service training of students and young leaders was also a key factor.

Kiamu and his team intentionally mentored young men and women. Titus Davis began as a church member and successively became the youth leader, associate pastor, senior pastor, EFCWA secretary, associate president, and then president. Gospel movements mentor and develop leaders from within. Davis personally mentored eight emerging leaders. Most of them pursued formal theological studies in Liberia, and two did masters-level training in Nigeria. But the key to the movement is not in developing professionals, but in informal training accessible to all. "It must be a layperson's movement," Davis affirms.

Partnerships also played a role. Meridian University equipped all the EFCWA workers in orality methods and disciple making. Missionary organizations helped them develop contextual training. Partner churches and organizations from the West contributed financially to equipping events, conferences, and gatherings for strategic planning. The involvement of ex-patriate missionaries and churches has made a difference in the movement.

Stage Four: Global Participation

The story of the EFCWA is a story of what God can do with people who have few resources but great vision and faith. The EFCWA sent out its first missionary to Sierra Leone in 2006. They gave him some goats to support himself and asked him to develop other workers and help them by sharing the fruit of his herd. Kiamu and Davis served as catalysts supporting the missionary efforts in Sierra Leone and other countries.

The Church Multiplication movement expanded to other West African nations using CMT to form partnerships and identify UPGs. As of 2018, CMT had moved across six generations of reproduction. The first generation saw sixteen churches emerge in Monrovia, Liberia. The second generation extended the church-planting efforts from that country to Sierra Leone, Guinea, and Ivory Coast. The third generation went from Guinea to Senegal, and the fourth is going from Senegal to Ghana, Gambia, and Guinea Bissau. Most recently, the EFCWA has begun work in Burkina Faso.

In 2020, the student who started the fourth church of the EFCWA, Titus Davis, led a network of approximately seven hundred churches in West Africa—two hundred with buildings and five hundred house churches. Twenty-three years after two students started that first church near the fish market, EFCWA has become a missionary-sending movement impacting thirteen West African countries. Liberians were the pioneers in this case, but Western missionaries came alongside them as mentors and teachers. Catalysts do not draw attention to themselves. They are content to pour their lives into local leaders who model multiplication.

Growth Challenges

The EFCWA movement is not without shortcomings. Davis asserts: "When a movement grows as rapidly as this one has, there are always growing pains." Systems and resources have not kept pace with the rate of growth, and without adequate support systems, discipleship efforts are inconsistent. Some regional leaders are hesitant to step out of their local pastorates to devote more time to mission and training. Resources are tight. The churches are autonomous and are required to find their own resources. They learn to rely on God, help each other, and rarely look to the national organization for direction or finances.

However, the greatest need is for more workers. Leadership is in short supply, and it is hard to keep up with the growing need for church planters, pastors, lay leaders, and movement leaders. Davis believes that movement growth will continue if they can make every disciple a disciple maker. That is the DNA of gospel movements. Discipleship is the thread that runs through movements and every growth stage—the very soil in which movements grow.

These stages of movement maturity serve as a lens to discern a movement's progress, but they do not explain the thrust of gospel movements. Their emergence comes from their spiritual vitality, the Spirit-given passion and propulsion of believers who desperately desire to know Christ and make him known. The culture in which they live and grow is a *discipleship culture*. Gospel movements have a discipleship DNA—they grow from an internal pattern of reproduction—disciples making disciples over generations. That pattern often makes the difference between a short-lived awakening and the birth of a movement. In the chapter that follows we look at several movements to explore the key to movement growth—instilling a discipleship DNA from the start.

7

Pathway to Movement Growth

James Edwin Orr has documented revivals that lead to church planting and missionary sending. However, we know from church history that not all awakenings produce movements. Some revitalize existing churches doctrinally and morally without creating a surge in church planting and missions. Renewal without mission often signals the lack of a discipleship culture.

The message which transforms lives, also compels witnesses. The Spirit that regenerates also calls and sends witnesses to the world. Thus, gospel movements are also discipling movements in which Christ-followers are made, matured, and multiplied. That discipling impetus carries the movement across generations, through challenges, and leadership transitions.

When it comes to CPMs, much focus has been placed on size and numbers. Smith has observed that every successful CPM movement has three qualitative dimensions:[1]

- A spiritual posture—abiding in Christ and relying on his wisdom and power to do the work. Leaders and members are filled by the Holy Spirit and walk in him.

- A simple discipleship pathway toward maturity and reproduction. Established Christians know how to help new believers grow in Christ and make other disciples.

1. Smith, "Finishing the Task."

- A process of reproduction that helps disciples follow the pathway and make other disciples. Disciples become disciple makers, resulting in reproducing church fellowships.

These common elements all flow from a discipleship mindset or culture.

DISCIPLESHIP CULTURE

Discipleship culture describes a way of thinking and living centered on being a follower of Jesus and making other followers. Generational reproduction (disciples make disciples who make other disciples) becomes the growth engine of gospel movements. The fact that most disciples in the West rarely reproduce must make us wonder if we have not lost an essential part of what it means to be Jesus' disciple.

"Christianity without the living Christ is inevitably Christianity without discipleship, and Christianity without discipleship is always Christianity without Christ."[2] Jesus called followers to come and die, not merely to make a commitment to change. This kind of Christian life is impossible humanly but becomes "normal" through the living, indwelling Spirit of Christ. If the six leading indicators of spiritual vitality (chap. 5) give us the spiritual temperature of a movement, disciple and leader reproduction speak most eloquently of the movement's culture. Movement leaders must not only live and model spiritual disciplines, but also create discipling pathways and equip all serious followers of Jesus to reproduce. In this we must go back to our roots.

The early church grew and spread throughout the Roman world in four decades largely because the early disciples, filled with the Spirit, obeyed their Savior, and made disciples as a way of life. According to historian Michael Green, ordinary disciples fueled the movement expansion: "This must often have been not formal preaching, but the informal chattering to friends and chance acquaintances . . . They went everywhere gossiping the gospel; they did it naturally, enthusiastically, and with the conviction of those who are not paid to say that sort of thing."[3]

Seeding is a biblical metaphor for disciple reproduction (Matt 13; John 12:24; 1 Cor 3:6). Roland Allen contended that "if the church is to be indigenous it must spring up in the soil from the very first seeds planted."[4] Tom Julien uses another agricultural metaphor for this culture of reproduction:

2. Bonhoeffer, *Cost of Discipleship*, 59.
3. Green, *Evangelism Early Church*, 173.
4. Allen, *Spontaneous Expansion*, 2.

In nature, seeds grow into plants that produce new seeds that in turn are to be planted. In the same way, the church is planted in culture so that it can produce seeds that will ensure its reproduction. We fulfill the Great Commission as we are faithful in planting seeds that are capable of growing into reproducing churches.[5]

Generational reproduction provides a root system that keeps on expanding. Wild strawberry plants and wild banana trees naturally expand underground by sending offshoots that produce new plants. This is more than a clever strategy. It was our Lord's master plan. His final command to his disciples was to go and make other disciples and to teach them everything he taught them, which includes the responsibility to make new disciples.

No Church Reproduction without Disciple Reproduction

Seeds have amazing reproductive capacity. I once asked a group of Chinese church planters about the reproductive capacity of an apple. One of them answered, "Eightfold, because each apple has eight seeds." Another chimed in, "It is unlimited, because each seed can produce an apple tree that will produce many apples, and so on." When we talked about the obstacles to reproduction, one confessed, "We never reproduced. We consumed the apple and all the seeds along with it." Reproduction is difficult in consumer societies. But it thrives where the biblical discipling practices that follow are present and growing.

- Prayer and evangelism form the point of the spear that extends gospel movements. Often acts of service that show Jesus' love and power accompany the verbal message.

- Baptism and grounding new believers in the faith follow without delay, primarily in households or within natural groupings and relational networks.

- Fellowships of disciples are formed wherever meeting places are found. Believers commit themselves to Jesus, to his teaching, to his mission, and to each other.

- Spirit-filled leaders are identified and empowered to provide care, equipping and leadership to new fellowships.

5. Julien, "ACT Strategy," 2.

- The disciples live distinctively and compassionately as communities of faith and witness, not isolated but serving others and bringing transformation as salt and light.

- These disciple-making communities also raise up and send workers to future harvest fields to repeat the pattern there.

Earlier we described the discipling process toward multiplication with the words *evangelize, establish, equip,* and *expand.* We use "discipleship" in the broadest sense, of the lifelong spiritual journey in Christlikeness and service to God. This broad use of the word "disciple" is consistent in Scripture. For example, in Acts 14, the Greek word "disciple" is used in the same narrative for new converts (v. 21), recent believers (v. 23) and mature Christians (v. 28). Discipleship is a lifetime call. Discipleship and leadership development are not separate tasks. They should be seen as a continuum with leaders emerging from the community of growing disciples so that disciples are made, matured, and multiplied.

Not all disciples will become church or missional leaders. Leaders have additional skills and capacity to develop and influence others. They are chosen, called, and gifted to the church by God (Eph 4:11–13). Nevertheless, even the most successful must remember that leading is what they do, but "disciple" describes who they are. Moral lapses, and many leadership breakdowns, are rooted in a failure of discipleship.

Leaders are not called to "shine" but to edify the church and to contribute to its mission. The most important ministry of leaders is not to use their gifting with excellence, or to have a great impact, but to apprentice others so that the church grows and reproduces.

> Whatever a person's ministry, one should always seek to reproduce asking, "Whom can I equip to do this ministry, who will be able to equip others also?" This is the key to multiplying transformational churches: evangelists reproducing evangelists, teachers reproducing teachers, church planters reproducing church planters, pastors reproducing pastors, missionaries reproducing missionaries. This will lead to collective reproduction of cell groups reproducing cell groups, and churches reproducing churches, ultimately leading to transformational movements.[6]

We also see this New Testament multiplication cycle (figure 7.1) in gospel movements today.

---

6. Ott, *Church on Mission,* 116–17.

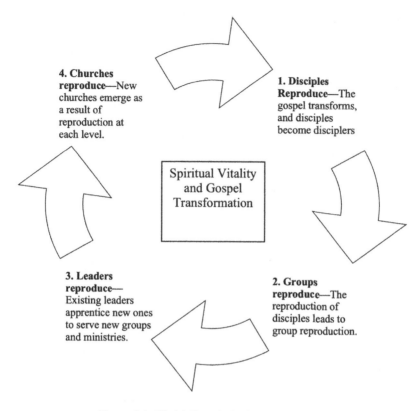

Figure 7.1. *Disciple Reproduction in the Book of Acts*

God's activity in this world is broader than discipling. He upholds widows, brings justice to the oppressed, cares for orphans, appoints rulers, and brings them down. Yet, making disciples is the central mandate he gave his followers, the pattern we see in Acts, and the DNA of gospel movements. For decades, intentional discipling had been relegated to parachurch organizations and ministries that specialize in an affinity group like Child Evangelism, Youth for Christ, Teen Challenge, CRU, or Navigators. For gospel movements to emerge, biblical discipling, captured in the principles that follow, must retake center stage in our churches and engage all believers, not just professionals.

No Multiplication without Mobilization

Not everyone is called to be a pastor or missionary, but everyone is called to be on mission with God. Mobilizing and preparing everyday people as disciple makers may sound like a novel idea, but it is not. The first gospel movements were not started by professional scribes or rabbis trained in the scholastic institutions of their day. Except for Saul of Tarsus, they were everyday people without theological education—fishermen, tradesmen, and businessmen transformed by the living Christ. The religious leaders of the day were astonished by the courage and authority of "unschooled and ordinary" men and women who had been with Jesus (Acts 4:13). Church history also attests to the untapped potential of nonprofessional gospel agents. According to church historian LaTourette, "The chief agents in the expansion of Christianity appear not to have been those who made it a profession or made it a major part of their occupation, but men and women who carried on their livelihood in some purely secular manner and spoke of their faith in this natural fashion."[7]

Another historian, W. R. Ward, calls this *priesthood of all believers* the Cinderella of all Protestant doctrines because of its surprising power to propel evangelical movements.[8] Then and now, the mobilization of nonformal disciple makers is a central element of gospel movements. Strachan, former director of the Latin America Mission, observed the remarkable expansion of new religious movements in the majority world and found that mobilization was a common thread to their success. His central thesis became: "The successful expansion of any movement is in direct proportion to its success in mobilizing and occupying its total membership in constant propagation of its beliefs."[9] Davis from Liberia said it well: "We will be successful if we make every disciple a disciple maker."

No Mobilization without Transformation

In gospel movements, it is not only a question of propagating a belief system but shaping character and changing lives. Transformed people become instruments of transformation. No mere strategy or program can provide the disciple-making mobilization that the Evangelical Free Church of West Africa (EFCWA) is experiencing. Discipleship is God's process of life transformation and Christians must themselves be transformed before they can bring transformation to others.

Discipleship includes a *renovation process* that starts with the heart and mind and leads to a new lifestyle of love and obedience. We should never trivialize discipleship by oversimplifying it. It is a lifelong journey involving

7. LaTourette, *First Five Centuries*, 117.

8. Ward, *Protestant Evangelical Awakening*, 353.

9. Peters, *Saturation Evangelism*, 51.

deliverance from bondage and worldview change through the Word and the Spirit. The way disciples are made will vary according to context and culture but discipling that leads to transformation and multiplication is most often *incarnational, relational,* and *transferable.*

Incarnational More Than Attractional

Ted Esler, president of MissioNexus, contrasts nonformal discipling with the traditional approach of making disciples prevalent in North America. The traditional view assumes that Christians who participate faithfully in the programs and ministries of a healthy church, led by a godly shepherd, will naturally grow as disciples. Their motto is: "Come to our church, get involved, and you will grow." If that is the discipling pathway, then the best way to make disciples is to attract people and get them plugged in. This describes the *attractional*—as opposed to the incarnational—approach. The watchword is *come,* rather than *go.* Discipleship simply happens naturally through faithful involvement in church activities.[10]

Is being a faithful church member enough? In the 1990s, leaders who saw that the churches were not experiencing conversion growth, began to question the effectiveness of the attractional model. Advocates of the disciple-making church, like Bill Hull and Rick Warren, restructured the church to make disciples *intentionally.* They issued a call to recover discipleship as the lifeblood of the church and to create intentional disciple-making pathways. They even challenged churches to evaluate all their programs, spending, and activities based on their discipling impact. This was a significant step forward. However, the discipleship focal point and culture did not change. Discipling was still centered in the church building and its programs and seekers were expected to leave their social world to become disciples. "Unfortunately, the focus of most disciple making has been on the structure of the church (the tool or tactic) that is doing the planting, not the community where the planting is being done."[11]

In our post-Christian secularizing societies, more incarnational discipling is needed. Missiologist Donald McGavran observed that often "resistance arises primarily from fear that 'becoming a Christian will separate me from my people.'"[12] The *incarnational* approach does not require that seekers leave their familiar environment, but that Christians engage them

---

10. Esler, "Coming to Terms," 68.

11. Watson, *Contagious Disciple Making,* 30.

12. McGavran, *Understanding Church Growth,* 191.

outside the church building—in neighborhoods, malls, clubs, schools, businesses, and other common spaces.

This is the norm in pioneer settings and places with anti-conversion laws. Some in the West are awakening to the need of a quantum shift that would move discipling into the harvest field both geographically and culturally. The secularizing societies of our post-Christian cities demand no less.

This does not mean that seekers should be kept away from the fellowship of believers. Both *come strategies* and *go strategies* can be used (see table 7.1). However, seekers should not have to dress differently, use new vocabulary, or sing strange songs to follow Christ. Eventually, disciples will be integrated into the church and learn a new way of thinking and acting, but transformation should begin on their *home turf.* Home Bible studies, DBS, and Bible storying are powerful and reproducible tools that can be taken to people where they are.

Table 7.1
Contrast between Attractional and Incarnational Discipleship

Attractional Discipleship	Incarnational Discipleship
The starting point for making disciples is the church, its leaders, resources, and strategies.	The starting point is the seeker's situation within society, his or her needs, brokenness, and aspirations.
Discipling happens in the context of the local church. Healthy churches produce healthy disciples.	The church happens in the context of local discipling. Healthy disciples produce healthy churches.
Church-centered. The discipleship culture is shaped by the church doing the church planting.	Society-centered. The discipleship culture is shaped by an understanding of the people group to be discipled.
Requires that seekers enter another culture to start their journey as disciples.	Requires that disciple makers meet seekers within their culture to help them start their journey.

More Relational Than Programmatic

The first disciples followed the pattern Jesus had established with them. Making disciples was life-on-life with an emphasis on relationships rather than programs. Programs are managed; people are loved. Programs are resource driven and last if personnel and finances are available. Relationships shine when they require sacrifice. Relational disciple making may not be the most efficient or easiest approach, but it is the timeless one that Jesus modeled.

Why is his approach universally relevant? Relationships are valued in all societies. They are simple and do not require finances, technology, or complex structures. Jesus' example as an itinerant teacher and full-time disciple maker may be hard to follow in our fast-paced society and compartmentalized lives. However, the principle remains: disciples are made through relationships that connect people to Jesus and to each other.

Transferable, Not Exceptional

Relational discipling is a universal and transferable model. Discipling becomes transferable when new Christians learn to feed themselves spiritually, grow their relationship to God, and help others do the same. Disciple makers model and teach how to know him, hear his voice, receive his teaching, respond in prayer, grow in trust, and share with neighbors.

Wise disciple makers will not make others dependent on their exceptional teaching or wisdom, but will help the new believer develop simple, but consistent, spiritual disciplines (prayer, Bible reading, worship, witness, and fellowship). They point to the Word and Holy Spirit as teachers and help others discover the plain meaning the text by asking questions (discovery method). The goal should be to always move toward self-nurture, reproduction, and mutual edification in community groups.

GROWING A DISCIPLESHIP CULTURE

A disciple-making movement is the fruit of generational disciple making. The age of a large tree can be determined accurately only by an actual count of the annual growth rings on a cross section of the stump. If gospel movements were giant sequoias, the growth rings would represent generations of disciples. Attempting to reproduce churches without a rhythm of disciples making others is doomed to disappoint.

When the iron curtain fell in Eastern Europe, many missionary organizations became involved in post-Communist Eurasia. Sensing that the window of opportunity would not last, the Alliance for Saturation Church Planting brought together some key players to develop CPMs by training a new wave of church planters. The alliance worked for thirteen years and accomplished some significant objectives. It provided research, encouragement, and learning.

One of its most notable contributions was the *Omega Course,* a decentralized equipping program to develop and deploy church planters and accelerate church planting. Yet, after thirteen years they dissolved the alliance (although some member organizations continued its work). Lee Behar, former executive director of the alliance, concluded that, although they had a well-balanced program to develop planters, they had failed to generate CPMs for two primary reasons.

First, there was an issue of selection. They found that teaching church planting does not make church planters. Many of those who went through the *Omega Course* were pastors who did not have the gifts and calling to plant churches, so, although many were trained, only a fraction ended up starting new churches.

The other lesson is that training must be part of something bigger. Church planting that does not have at its root a disciple-making movement will not yield a CPM. Church-planter development must flow from a disciple-making environment. A constant supply of leaders is needed for churches to multiply. That supply must come from a regular stream of new disciples.

> Spiritual movement of any kind is not possible outside of an environment of disciple-making. Church planting is no exception. In order for churches to be multiplied, leaders must be multiplied. Multiplying leaders requires multiplying disciples and multiplying disciples can only come through fruitful evangelism. We who believe that saturation church planting is the best way to fulfill the Great Commission must always remember that it is only a vehicle that fulfills the task if disciples are being made and multiplied. We must never take this truth for granted.[13]

The pattern must be intentional and established early. When we launch new churches by gathering Christians, without reaching and discipling the lost, we put off the all-important mission of instilling a discipleship culture. The unintended message is that making disciples can wait, and that the most rapid path to a critical mass of worshipers is what counts. Movements establish a foundation of discipling from the start. Establishing a discipleship pattern before launching worship services may not be the easiest path but changing the church culture has usually proven even more challenging.

13. Behar, "Reflection," 2.

RECOVERING A DISCIPLESHIP CULTURE

If discipling, that is reproducible and transformative, is the DNA of gospel movements, why are there so few examples of it in the Western world? Despite the abundant theological, technical, and financial advantages at their disposal, few Western church groups approach the 10 percent average annual rate of growth seen in Communist China, Hindu Nepal, and Roman Catholic Central America. Few achieve even 5 percent growth. Many are barely holding their own or are losing ground. David Garrison and Ed Stetzer, two respected missiologists, bemoan the lack of CPMs in the Western world.

> We are haunted by the reality that CPMs have transpired on North American soil previously when America was a developing nation itself. Between 1795 and 1810, the Baptists and the Methodists won the Western frontier in what can be characterized as the only effective CPM ever to occur in the United States. The questions arise then: Why haven't we seen it since? And is the answer due to other external factors that have yet to be adapted to or dismantled, or is it simply that nobody in the US has even tried to create the environment for a true CPM?[14]

Stetzer and Garrison conclude that there is no quick fix, no silver bullet. On the contrary, some deeply entrenched traditions and tightly held values would have to change for more gospel movements to occur in the Western world.[15]

One hindrance is the *complexity of church life* in the West. Christians from other countries who visit a North American Evangelical church are often positively impressed. The worship is orderly and inspiring. The website lists a vast array of opportunities and services to members. The preacher, a trained and skilled expositor, has spent many hours preparing the sermon. The facilities are impeccable, and the welcome offered to visitors is second to none. So, what's the problem? Occasionally, success becomes an enemy. This type of complex church, exceptional by global standards, requires highly gifted ministers and salaried staff, and is difficult to plant or reproduce.

> By virtue of girth, large churches demand a high level of complexity merely to operate and require a massive expenditure of energy and resources in order to expand. Often, the complexity of its systems hinders its ability to multiply and instead co-opts a disciple-making mission into a volunteer placement agency.

14. Stetzer and Garrison, "Church Planting Movements," 1.

15. For more on this question, see Trousdale and Sunshine, *Kingdom Unleashed*.

Hundreds of mini roles are scheduled and staffed in order to deliver on the values of extraordinary excellence. It becomes very expensive addition. But perhaps its highest price cannot be calculated in simple monetary terms, but in the effect that the "extraordinary excellence" has had on the church's ability to produce multiplying disciples. Addition cannot easily be upgraded to multiplication because of the level of leader required to run the machinery.[16]

A closely related obstacle to gospel movement is the *reliance on professional ministry* including pastoral salaries, special buildings, licensing requirements, and theological degrees. The problem is not with the quality of ministry but with the expectation that ministers *must be* vocationally trained. Meaning to do well and set high standards, proponents of professionalism in ministry add qualifications, beyond the biblical requirements of calling, gifting, and character. Extrabiblical requirements impose unnecessary burdens and disempower many willing and gifted servants. These "extras" come at a price, as they reduce the Christian workforce, impede momentum, and stifle multiplication.

> When we lose the priesthood of believers, we lose massive impact for the gospel . . . Churches should not merely empower the laity (as in a team mission situation) but empower the indigenous laity—the local believers who come to faith in Christ should function in a priestly role themselves, the role of bringing their own lost families and friends to Christ. True reproduction occurs when people are given permission to function as God has gifted and directed.[17]

Thirdly, the Western church is too often plagued by a *consumer mentality*. Most Christians "attend church" to be fed; they expect to receive rather than to be equipped to make a difference in their world. For gospel movements to cover the landscape with disciple-making communities, the DNA of multiplication must be recovered, starting with nonformal discipling. Developing fully devoted followers of Jesus must once again become our central focus, even if it involves personal cost and sacrifice. To revive this discipling momentum, two major shifts are needed. First, people in the pews must rediscover their calling as kingdom agents, sent and equipped with spiritual gifts and power. Second, those in the pulpits must assume their responsibility as equippers who model, prepare, and empower their people for the work of the ministry rather than doing it all themselves (Eph 4:11).

16. Christopherson, "What Comes After Church Growth?," para. 9.

17. Stetzer and Garrison, "Church Planting Movements," 15.

Disciple making as the pathway to growth can be recovered, but the better course of action is to establish it from the start. The following case study from one of the most broken regions of the world should give us hope and direction. God is growing a gospel movement with incarnational disciple making as a central focus in the slums of Brazil.

CAJU LIFE CHURCH—A DISCIPLE-MAKING FELLOWSHIP

Fabio Ramos Silva grew up in a Christian home and attended a middle-class church in Rio de Janeiro, Brazil. His father instilled in him a heart for by-passed, forgotten people. Close to their home, there was a favela, a haphazard patchwork of colorful shacks forming a working-class shantytown. Favelas are rudimentary homes put up hastily by squatters who do not own the land. They rise and spread rapidly like wild plants. When Fabio was only sixteen, he joined his father in serving the people of this forgotten neighborhood. Later, when he graduated from Bible school, he faced a choice—become the youth pastor at a comfortable middle-class church, or resurrect a struggling little church plant in Caju, a favela in the port area of Rio.

In 2005, after working for a year in a traditional church, Fabio chose to serve the needy of Caju. In this blue-collar district, people work in the cement industry and handle cargo containers for the nearby port, but jobs are scarce. Crime, poverty, drugs, and the lack of education make it a difficult place in which to live and work. Yet Fabio, just twenty-three years old, moved in with Lia, his young wife, to grow the fledgling church plant.

When he expressed his vision to share God's love with the broken-hearted in the streets, five of the seven church members left. With the two that remained, the couple began reaching out to neighbors with the gospel. They cared for the neediest and brought some of them into their home. They shared words of hope as they helped one person and one family at a time. Life in the favela was a collection of extended families, living close to each other in modest apartments. Fabio says: "When you win someone, you win all the family's problems." The young church showed the difference Christ makes, and the gospel spread along relational lines.

Fabio and friends soon realized that they would not see individuals and families transformed unless they addressed the community problems that permeated Caju. Drug traffickers ruled the street and exacted protection money from the struggling merchants. Young people were sucked into a life of petty thievery or drug trafficking to survive. Few finished high school, and even fewer got a college education. People wanted to escape Caju but could not make it on their own.

The young couple faithfully prayed and visited people in the street and in homes. One day, when someone was healed through prayer, a small revival broke out. The extended family believed, and 80 percent of their neighbors came to Christ. Then the word started to spread that God was doing something new in Caju. Disciples and home discipling groups multiplied from that point forward.

Movement Growth Factors

Evangelism and discipling were the greatest contributors to movement growth. The vision, *win-establish-disciple-send*, provided the church with a discipling pathway and continues to be the driving force behind church growth. Multiplication takes place at the level of the home groups. New house churches are started by natural extension as the home groups reproduce. The following discipling elements were most significant as the church grew from four to four hundred adults with fifty life groups and two daughter churches in ten years.[18]

- The quality and zeal in evangelism and discipling.
- The loving lifestyle and genuine care of Christians for those around them.
- The use of life groups to reach the lost, disciple believers, and provide community.
- The courage and care of the spiritual shepherds.

Blessing through Evangelism and Social Action

Evangelism is the primary impetus behind this gospel movement. Everything they do contributes directly or indirectly to helping people come to Christ and grow in him. The Caju church uses both incarnational and attractional approaches. They share the good news directly and indirectly. They would say with the Apostle Paul: "To the weak I became weak, that I

---

18. The life groups function as basic Christian communities and meet the requirements to be considered house churches. This is why we consider this a gospel movement of four generations in less than twenty years.

might gain the weak: I am become all things to all men, that I may by all means save some" (1 Cor 9:22). Below are some examples (table 7.2).

Table 7.2
Holistic Evangelism of the Caju Church

Indirect Evangelism	Direct Evangelism
Marriage intervention and help	Tract distribution
Food distribution	Street marches with public evangelism
Literacy efforts with children	Harvest day festival with fun and games
Psychological care	Evangelism during Carnival time
People brought to drug recovery center	Home visits to church visitors
Sick visited at home and in the hospital	Personal, lifestyle evangelism

These efforts work together. The process of transformation usually takes several points of connection that build on each other: a need, a conversation, a social gathering, a prayer group, and, finally, an invitation to follow Jesus at a gathering. Those who come forward soon join a life group and receive mentoring by a more mature Christian. Fabio and the Caju church do not wait until people become converted to start discipling them. They go to them, bless them, invite them to a group, expose them to Jesus through his Word and fellowship. In Caju, "blessing and belonging" usually come before "believing and becoming."

Life and Community Transformation

After two years, sixty people were meeting in home-based life groups during the week and in a rented facility for worship on Sundays. Most were first-generation Christians under thirty years old. One of their burdens was the drug problem. Fabio asked, "Could God make Caju drug-free for even twenty-four hours?" The young church prayed and promoted the idea. Nine other churches joined them. A new kingpin had taken over the drug cartel. Fabio went to see him and told him about their campaign—a day without drugs. The man did not object, so Fabio clarified: "That means you will put the word out that no one is to sell drugs that day?" He accepted.

Fabio recruited other churches to pray and prepare for the drug-free day. When it finally came, three hundred volunteers went out on the streets, praising God and declaring his power. They confronted a dealer who did not *get the memo* and asked him to stay off the streets. He went home, put on his best clothes, and came back to take part in the event. Drug dealing continued, but it no longer ruled the streets.

Then the government started a different kind of war on drugs. They fought fire with fire by sending in hit squads to take down dealers. During this battle, the church did not abandon its street presence and witness. Life groups were out every week, and a large rally took place once a month. On special occasions, hundreds marched through the district, forming an evangelistic parade for Christ that openly praised God. This continued for years.

In 2005, Craig Weyandt, a missionary and church-planting catalyst, was told about the Caju church and tried to contact them; but he didn't feel safe going into their neighborhood alone. Fabio had heard of Craig's interest and sent two Christian ladies to get him. They met him at a gas station on the outskirts of the favela and walked him in. When Craig met Fabio for the first time, it was the start of a very special relationship. On one occasion, Craig and some friends were caught in the crossfire of two rival gangs. Terrified, they crouched in a corner. Fabio came to the rescue with other worshippers and got them out of the line of fire.

Local Discipling and Life Groups

There are many megachurches in Brazil. Most attract crowds with their charismatic leadership, passionate preaching, and invigorating worship. Fabio is a staid, reflective, and single-minded leader who models what he expects of others—following Christ at any cost. From the start, he determined that they would build the church through gospel transformation and intentional discipling. As a result, they deliberately grounded those who came to Christ in the Word and lovingly taught them to walk with Christ.

In the Caju movement, life group leaders care for those in their spiritual family and make sure they are mentored. They call the initial follow-up "establishing." This step clarifies the commitment and prepares new believers for baptism. Once baptized, they equip them to witness to their family and friends and become disciple makers. In this discipling process they become part of a life group and attend Sunday evening worship services. Those who come to the worship service have, for the most part, already heard the gospel in a home or on the street. Thus, the public services become a place to harvest the fruit from personal evangelism. The goal is to see life groups expand outwardly and form new networks. Then the new network finds a rented place in which to meet for larger celebrations.

By 2005, when Craig visited the church, it had grown to 120 people. Only half could be seated; the other half spilled over into the street. Then they rented and renovated a dilapidated, two-floor warehouse. Craig suspected that they would ask for financial help, but they did not. Members contribute according to their ability, using the skills and resources at their disposal. On the stage, a sign reads, "The law of discipleship—If anyone wants to be my disciple, he must deny himself, take up his cross daily and follow me" (Luke 9:23).

Local Transformation and Multiplication

The church served the community in many ways, besides combatting drugs. Voluntary tutors helped high schoolers graduate and go on to university. Those who had small businesses provided work opportunities. The church sent representatives to the prefecture to work with them on improving basic health and public lighting. Life groups cared for the sick and visited the hospitalized.

In 2006, 250 more people joined the Caju church fellowship so that, a year after they moved in the warehouse, four hundred people were involved in life groups. They asked if they could build a meeting place on a piece of land used during the week as a sports complex. The Christian NGO that owned part of it gave them permission, but a local drug lord took over the property. The leaders prayed and went to see him. He agreed to let them use it for a pittance because "they were helping the people." Initially, they put up a tin roof on a wooden frame without walls. Then, little by little, they completed the building project. By 2008, the church had grown to five hundred, with fifty leaders in training.

Fabio oversaw the development and care of church leaders, pastors, and missionaries with the help of other mature leaders. Their leadership development program includes on-the-job experience and mentoring or coaching. One quarter of the current leaders supplement their hands-on training with classes at a local Bible school. Others receive in-service training, a leadership development course, practical workshops, and mentoring on-the-job.

Church planting is one of their strongest values, after compassion ministry, evangelism, discipleship, and life groups. They have seen four generations of reproduction in their life groups, which are basic Christian communities. Pastors shepherd the existing groups and lay planters start new ones. The lay planters share the gospel every day, follow the church-planting process, pray for believers regularly, disciple them, and prepare good resources for them. They are accountable to one another and to the pastors. They start life groups and move on after identifying, promoting, and mentoring a pastoral leader from within the new life group. Finally, they turn over authority to him or her and the new pastor shepherds the flock, leads in mission, and oversees the formation of new groups.

Life groups typically start with about seven members, grow to thirty, and reproduce. They send missionary teams out to establish new ones. Craig explained that the multiplication process is not controlled by Fabio. Life groups can reproduce without prior approval. What was once a struggling congregation, by 2009, had become a legal church called Igreja Vida Caju. Caju Life Church has also started two churches, one in a Rio de Janeiro district called Nova Iguaçu, and the other in Parnaiba, in northeastern Brazil.

The distant work in Parnaiba started when a Caju church life group leader returned there and started evangelizing and discipling family and friends. He also led an "encounter with God" group—an intensive weekend of deliverance and life transformation. When a local church-planting pastor saw the fruit of this lay couple's ministry, he invited them to introduce discipleship and life groups to his fledgling church plant. The impact was such that the church grew and joined the Caju movement. Ever since then, groups from Caju have been traveling north to lend a hand in Parnaiba, one of the poorest areas of the country.

Crisis and Adjustments

The work started when Fabio was only twenty-three and grew quickly among young singles and newly marrieds. They poured all their energy into evangelism, helping people, and discipling new believers. A dozen years later, at this writing, the vision has not changed but the realities have. Life is becoming more complex, and the church is having to adjust. The initial disciples are now in their mid-thirties, and most are married with several elementary-age kids. The church is working through growing pains, going from an informal fellowship of young adults to a church family of five hundred adults with different needs, and a growing number of children of all ages. The congregation has initiated ministries like marital counseling, family life preparation, and Christian education. Life group pastors are assuming more responsibility to lead the ministries and care for various age groups. As a result, street evangelism and compassion ministry have slowed down as more time and energy is invested internally.

These are difficult times in Rio. According to Craig, 56 percent of all Brazilians polled would leave the country if they could. Rio has suffered from economic and security crises more than most cities. Economic realities are putting pressure on the movement. To prepare for the Olympics, the owners of the building used for worship more than doubled the rent. Many members of the Caju church are without jobs. To make matters worse, several drug cartels moved back in and compete for business. Crime is on the rise once again, and violence is taking its toll on church leaders. Many, including Fabio himself, have been held up at gunpoint.

One of the young ladies that Fabio and Lia invested in married a Macumba priest who savagely, in a demonic fit, bludgeoned her to death. The church was left to care for the children. Fabio came to collect their passports and other belongings. The emotional stress of all of this has taken a toll on him and his family.

The movement that was focused on the broken lives of Caju is gaining a vision beyond the favela. The churches are continuing faithfully, and other leaders have stepped into the vacuum. Organization has improved. Members have inaugurated a school for the most vulnerable of children, many of whom have a drug trafficker for a mom or dad. The new school, administered by someone who came to Christ through the church, serves thirty children and is working toward adding thirty more. Craig is delighted: "We have seen kids and their families coming to Jesus and leave drug trafficking. Many children now can read and write!"[19]

The Impact of a Church Planting Catalyst

Starting a gospel movement is no *walk in the park*. Part of the discipleship culture is a culture of sacrifice and self-denial. The joy of seeing lives and families transformed cannot be denied, but the spiritual battle takes its toll. Craig and some friends graciously made it possible for Fabio and Lia to take a sabbatical in Portugal. I met up with Fabio there and listened to him share about his restoration and new vision for the future. They rested and returned from their sabbatical with renewed energy and a desire to send missionaries to North Africa.

Local leaders like Fabio need support and coaching. Craig became that person in Fabio's life. He started out as a single missionary doing surfing evangelism and helping on a church-planting team. Through the years, he saw that the greatest fruit, over time, came from investing in young emerging Brazilian leaders. He coached Fabio through good and trying times. He helped the church with leadership development and brought in several other equipping resources. He created a new network of church planters that is learning from the disciple-making experience of Fabio and Caju Life Church.

19. Weyandt, "Multiplying Transformational Churches," 1.

Catalysts like Craig are there when you need them. Chapter 8 offers the ideal profile of a catalyst. Few would claim to measure up completely and they need not. A catalyst is not an expert. God shapes catalysts in the thick of ministry. That was Craig's experience and that of the catalysts we will feature in the chapters that follow.

8

Profile of a Catalyst

Catalysts come alongside movement leaders to develop them and help them multiply healthy disciples, leaders, and churches. David Nicholas changed the spiritual landscape of South Florida and beyond before he went home to be with the Lord. He was a simple man who came from humble beginnings. He remained a pastor at the same church, Spanish River Presbyterian, in Boca Raton, Florida, for forty-two years. Yet, the impact of his life is felt throughout his country and in many others. He died on his fifty-second spiritual birthday in the same city where he came to Christ. He will always be an example to me of one in whom the gospel went deep and traveled far.

Nicholas was a church-planting catalyst who stayed put as a pastor, while he developed people for the multiplication of gospel churches. He had a singular passion for sharing the gospel which evolved into a passion for church planting. While the church grew to 1,800 people, with a fine Christian School, he was instrumental in starting 250 other churches. He cofounded the Acts 29 Network with Darrin Patrick, which has in turn founded and fostered many gospel-centered churches.[1] He mobilized his local church to be a training center, hosting many church-planting interns, and serving as the base for the Church Planting Network—a nonprofit dedicated to giving church planters a start both strategically and financially.[2]

1. Acts 29 is a global ministry with coordinators in ten regions and an eleventh coordinator for emerging regions that operates primarily in the Americas, Europe, Oceana, and South Africa (www.acts29.com).

2. The church planter internships at Spanish River Presbyterian are done in collaboration with Reformed Theological Seminary in Orlando, Florida.

Nicolas got involved personally, hosting groups of eight planters at a time, until he had personally mentored one hundred church planters.

Because of this singular focus, Spanish River Presbyterian is what you could call a great-grandfather of gospel-centered churches. By some accounts, it is considered the fifth most multiplying church in America, having produced more daughter churches than all but four other American churches. Moreover, its impact continues through its spiritual progeny because it sponsored the start of number one and number two on the list, Redeemer Presbyterian Church in New York founded by Tim Keller, and Mars Hill Church in Seattle founded by Mark Driscoll.[3]

The sponsoring of new churches and mentoring of church planters were very intentional. Nicholas stated: "To keep the ball rolling, we now mandate through our Church Planter's Covenant that the church planter will build a church that has church planting in its DNA."[4] Nicholas was gripped with the gospel and dedicated to seeing it transform communities through church planting. His death did not make the national headlines. He was first a local pastor and community leader who served his people. Nevertheless, in terms of multiplying churches, Nicholas and his associates at Spanish River Presbyterian are giants.

QUALITIES OF CATALYSTS

The word catalyst is formally used for a substance that permits or accelerates a chemical reaction (enzyme, reactant, synergist, catalytic agent, chemical reactor) or, more popularly, for a person or thing acting as a stimulus. In this book, a *church-planting catalyst* is an experienced church planter who invests in others to multiply disciples, leaders, and churches.

In chapter 5 we compared the work of catalysts to scaffolding. They exist to support the work of movement leaders. They do not create movement, but their contribution can accelerate and extend the reach of a movement. Nicholas's life underlines this principle: Gospel movements emerge because men and women, gripped with the gospel, multiply disciples and gospel-preaching churches.

Few people rise to Nicholas's stature—which leads us to ask, "Who qualifies to serve as a church-planting catalyst?" The following list comes by observing and interviewing dozens of catalysts. I compared my list to other profiles including a compilation made by Steve Smith, coauthor of the book

3. Kwon, "Top Multiplying Churches," para. 13.
4. Kwon, "Top Multiplying Churches," para. 14.

T4T. A Discipleship Re-Revolution.[5] While not exhaustive, it highlights the most salient qualities of catalysts. We invite you to do a personal inventory as you read on.

The Heart of a Catalyst—Being

The heart of the matter is a matter of the heart. Catalysts love God and others. The people they serve will tolerate many mistakes, if they know that the heart is right, as reflected in these candid comments made by movement leaders in East Africa:

> To be a DMM catalyst, come with less organizational inten-
> tion—have open hands to help the body, not to claim. You must
> have a Kingdom mindset. Releasing organizational control is
> essential for movement . . . An effective outside leader is not
> desperate to be everywhere in order to take credit. They are not
> high-profile . . . Control and ownership can kill a movement.
> Focus on empowering leaders and helping them to reach and
> develop their own organizations.[6]

Ministry That Flows from Identity in Christ

Catalysts have a kingdom mindset, meaning that they serve the King more than any cause or organization. The human institution is a means, not the end. Their focus is not personal achievement, rather, the fruitfulness of those in whom they invest. They reproduce themselves in others, always developing and empowering them to become all that God wants them to be. Like John the Baptist, they say, "I must decrease that he might increase." Believing that no one is beyond the reach of God's grace, they see poten-tial in the neglected, unwanted, and by-passed who want to follow Christ unconditionally.

Resolve and Resilience

Catalysts are known for their resolve—an unflinching commitment to doing whatever it takes to fulfill their Great Commission calling. They share the courage of Shadrach and his two companions who, when threatened with

5. Smith, "Profile of Movement Catalyst," 38–41.
6. Miller, "Role of Outsider Leaders," 17.

the fiery furnace, replied to King Nebuchadnezzar, "Our God will deliver us, *but if not*, still we will never bow down to your statue" (Daniel 3:17–18). Having counted the cost, catalysts consider their lives delivered into Christ's hands and dispensable in his service.

Resilience is resolve in the face of adversity, the ability to bounce back, to recover from setbacks, and to process discouragement so that it doesn't turn into despondency. Some are more resilient by nature—like the boxer who wins the fight on rounds because he keeps getting up. Others find their resilience not in temperament but in trust—like King David who, having lost his family and the support of his troops, "found his strength in the Lord his God" (1 Sam 30:6). He consulted God, caught up to the enemy, and fought them for twenty-four hours in the power that God provided. Those of us who have been involved in church planting, have learned, like David, to anchor hope in God and find strength in him.

Proven Character and Spiritual Vitality

Catalysts are gripped by the gospel, but fervor is not sufficient. Effective catalysts are trusted and respected men and women of proven character who manifest the fruit of the Spirit. They are people of prayer who seek the face of God and abide in him. A catalyst must meet biblical standards as do elders, deacons, and deaconesses (1 Tim 1; Titus 1; Acts 6). They have learned the art of self-leadership and show it through personal discipline. They are patient during the early phases of church planting and never stop doing the things that lead to disciple and church multiplication—even when they don't see immediate results. They are willing to be tested and humble enough to earn the trust of local leaders.

Vision and Faith

Steven Covey popularized the phrase "Begin with the end in mind." Garrison concurs, "The best place to begin your efforts is at the end, with the vision God has given you. Evaluate all you do in light of that vision."[7] The Watsons, pioneer missionaries to the Bhojpuri of India, asked themselves what it would take to reach ninety million in their generation.[8] That vision must come from God.

---

7. Garrison, *Church Planting Movements*, 278.

8. Watson, *Contagious Disciple Making*, 60.

Jesus told his disciples, "Blessed are those who have not seen, and yet have believed" (John 20:29). Catalysts are kingdom risk takers who believe that nothing attempted is nothing gained. They are futurists who live for something greater than themselves and envision gospel movements where there are none. They have two feet firmly planted on the ground, but dream of what could be, and work to that end. The martyred archbishop Oscar Romero expressed the empowering hope of those who see their frailty, accept their limitations, and know they are part of something greater.

> It helps now and then to step back and take a long view. The Kingdom is not only beyond our efforts; it is beyond our vision. We accomplish in our lifetime only a fraction of the magnificent enterprise that is God's work. Nothing we do is complete, which is another way of saying that the kingdom always lies beyond us . . . We may never see the end results, but that is the difference between the master builder and the worker. We are workers, not master builders, ministers, not messiahs. We are prophets of a future not our own.[9]

Catalysts look to what could be, rather than bemoaning what is still lacking. Because of this, they see the potential in people and invest in them. They are encouraging mentors, filled with hope, who regularly communicate God-centered possibilities.

The Head of a Catalyst—Knowing

Catalysts should be intellectually prepared. Paul and Barnabas navigated several cultures, but when they arrived in Lystra, they did not expect to be mistaken for Zeus and Hermes. The fickle crowd first worshipped them, then stoned Paul (Acts 14:8–20). There will always be surprises, but catalysts do their homework before engaging people cross-culturally. They should not only have a basic understanding of church-planting principles and best practices for multiplication, but also have a handle on the religion, worldview, and culture of those they are engaging.

A Movement Mindset

Catalysts have a movement mindset. They envision a gospel movement in their context. Because of this, they think in terms of multiplication rather than addition. They are not focused on planting a church, not even a great

9. Untener, "Prayer of Oscar Romero," 1.

church, but want to see churches reproduce and fill the land. They think generationally, meaning that, like Jesus, they concentrate on the few who are committed to reproduction, and invest faithfully in them. They mentor disciple makers, coach coaches, and train trainers. This was the case in Addis Ababa, where Alemayehu reproduced level-one church planter training twice of his own initiative after the initial training event was completed. He explained, "We did not have the right people. Those who attended your training were the official leaders, but I trained the reproducers."

People of Conviction Who Adapt to the Context

Catalysts have studied church planting and CPMs. But, most of all, they are people of the Word. They live in the book of Acts and ground their ministry in biblical principles and patterns. They have learned from their mistakes and have identified fruitful practices for multiplication. They are not easily distracted or deterred. Although they are shaped by their convictions, and not easily dissuaded, they are gracious when others disagree.

Catalysts have different personalities. Some are serious, with a laser-like focus; others are known for their sense of humor. But all need to be adaptable and resilient. Whether traveling to other cultures or serving in a multicultural city, effective catalysts learn and adjust along the way. They hold on to biblical essentials and adapt to the situation. Those who are formulaic or inflexible will surely struggle. Rigid people who believe that there is only one method, and that they have found it, don't make for good catalysts.

Catalysts as Eternal Learners

One common misconception is that only successful workers, with glowing records, become fruitful catalysts. James Joyce is reputed to have said that mistakes are the portal of discovery. Catalysts believe that to be true and don't waste their mistakes. Growing catalysts are continual learners, avid readers, and teachable partners. We have found that the best catalysts are those who learn well, not those for whom things come easily. Catalysts, especially those who work across cultures, listen and observe before trying to lecture or lead. They need an inquisitive and disciplined mind, always looking for cultural mentors, new models, and tools for their toolbox.

The Hands of a Catalyst—Doing

The order is important here: Heart, head, hands. People do not start out as catalysts. God touches their hearts and dispenses spiritual gifts when he calls his servants. They develop skills in the flow of ministry. As ministry grows, they learn to work in and through others, while they model personal prayer, evangelism, and discipling. They practice what they preach. They need not have a stellar track record, only the wisdom and credibility that come from experience.

Four-Fold Role of Catalysts

Juma, an African DMM catalyst asserts, "A paradigm shift that is needed for outside leaders is to realize that they cannot be involved in everything."[10] We have identified four primary roles that correspond to the support systems needed in CPMs: The catalyst as *trainer, coach, assessor,* and *mobilizer.* As soon as the first churches emerge, some form of people-development is needed. Leaders need to be trained and coached. Assessment will help to identify who is gifted as a pioneer planter and who should be a church strengthener. Then workers and teams need to be mobilized and equipped for new harvest fields (see chap. 10).

Ability to Contextualize

Some catalysts have a ministry description defined for them when they begin their ministry. They are given a strategic framework within which they operate.[11] Even in those cases, catalysts must apply the strategy to new contexts and develop tactics to fit the situation. Contextualization is a critical skill for anyone moving into a new culture with the gospel. A *person of peace* may look different from one context to the other. Catalysts help others look through the twin lenses of Scripture and local culture to prayerfully find bridges for the gospel to cross. They see each situation as a unique, God-given opportunity. They use illustrations and case studies from the region to share new ideas. These narratives, when used appropriately, are among the most transferable resources.

10. Miller, "Role of Outsider," 17.
11. Catalysts who work with DMM or T4T are examples of this.

The House of Catalysts—Relating

Catalysts need both hard skills (functional), and soft skills (relational). Most books and training focus on the former. But the ability to engage others, build trust, and communicate Christ's love will trump technical knowledge every day. Catalysts must enjoy getting to know people, savoring cultural differences, finding points of connection, and learning about local life. They must be open and authentic to take down walls of suspicion.

Making Time for Tea

To build a solid partnership one must sip many cups of tea or coffee. Trusting relationships are needed to bridge cultural misunderstandings and carry the weight of future strains. Catalysts are busy people. Many are task oriented— but they will never succeed unless they make time for people. Office-time should be limited, and people-time maximized. Catalysts develop the practices of mentoring and coaching. They invest in others by taking apprentices with them on ministry trips, observing them in action, and debriefing with them afterward. They are always thinking, who can I take along?

Open-Handed Relationships

Movement leaders need several voices in their lives. Catalysts should never be possessive in their relationships; nor should they feel slighted if a leader seeks the counsel of others. Although accountability is important, it works best if it is voluntary, within agreed-upon boundaries. This shows respect and trust. Passionate movement leaders tend to burn out or blow up over time. If a catalyst models genuineness and transparency, others will be more likely to share their struggles before conflict reaches the point of no return.

Hospitality and Generosity

"An overseer must be . . . hospitable" (1 Tim 3:2). Green affirms, "One of the most important methods of spreading the gospel in antiquity was the use of homes."[12] Today as well, God uses hospitality to further the gospel. Christians must have their house in order, not only as a testimony, but also so that their home can be a place of blessing, help and discipling. Catalysts often serve away from home, staying in guest homes or hotel rooms. Even

12. Green, *Evangelism in Early Church*, 207.

away from home, they can follow the Master's example of hospitality toward others (John 1:28–29). Acts of kindness like inviting a partner's family out for a meal speak loudly.

AN EMERGING CATALYST IN GERMANY

We love success stories with flashy numbers. They give us joy, but rarely paint an accurate picture of the difficult transitions needed to move toward multiplication. Timo Heimlich is helping church planters come together, and adopt new paradigms, to see a gospel movement take root in Berlin. He would be the first to say he has not arrived, but shared his journey and struggles, in the hope that others will learn from them.

Berlin, a world-class city of almost four million people, is the capital and largest city of Germany, both by population and size. For years a divided city, the base stones of the wall that separated free and occupied zones are still visible. Timo's vision is to see Berlin transformed through the gospel, filled with disciples and churches that bring transformation to every sphere of society.

After his studies at Moody Bible Institute, Timo went on to theological studies in Germany and a church-planting internship in Minneapolis. For the last fifteen years he has worked as a church planter, coach, and church-planting facilitator in Pankow, northeastern Berlin. Pankow is the most populous and the second-largest borough of Berlin. The work there is part of a coalition between the Freie Evangelische Gemeinde (FeG) or Free Evangelical Church of Germany, ReachGlobal Mission, and others. Together they launched the vision of thirty churches by 2020.

The realization of this vision has been more difficult than expected. Several new churches have been started by addition, rather than multiplication. By addition, we mean that a site is selected, and a church planter begins the work of raising support while building relationships in the community. Diet Schindler, former church-planting director of the FeG, has found that a church plant takes six years on average to become sustainable, and most church planters depend on funds from outside Germany. Why has progress been so slow?[13]

In the past, German Christians have expected their church planters to be theologically trained pastors with entrepreneurial leadership and excellent public speaking skills. These *pedigree* standards are expected because of the need to raise finances nationally and internationally. Planters travel

---

13. These are my observations and opinions, not Timo's, even though he read and approved the case study.

and speak broadly to raise support like missionaries. Prospective support-ing churches want to back a winner, a movement leader. Funds must also be raised for administrative help, gospel ministries, and a meeting place for worship. Organizations like *City-to-City*[14] connect these planters to po-tential donors. Others who aspire to plant a church often expect the same outside funding. This is a model of slow addition rather than multiplication.

Everyone would like a pedigree church planter; however, exceptional-ism is the enemy of multiplication. One German church planter shared that of the ten aspiring church planters in his seminary cohort, only three were able to raise adequate support. He finances himself as a corporate lawyer and dedicates as much time as he can to the church plant. He added that there were fifty attempts to plant churches in Frankfurt, between 2004 and 2014, and only three of those were continuing in March 2014.

The profile of the typical planter presents another challenge. Many of the church planters are pastoral leaders, rather than evangelists or pioneers. They naturally gravitate toward caring and growing the believers rather than meeting new people and sharing good news. While they can train church members in evangelism and discipleship, they may not be effective exam-ples. Their *professionalism*, an asset in many ways, creates the false narrative that you need special training to be a disciple-maker and that ministry is the domain of a few specialists, rather than the responsibility of all.

Berliners are among the most secular, post-Christian people in Eu-rope. They are resourceful, creative, and friendly for the most part; but they live Godless lives. One quarter of Berliners are not ethnic Germans, and the largest group, Turks of various origins, number one quarter of a million. They believe in a spirituality which is generated from within; not one that comes from above. An army of willing witnesses is needed, not a few profes-sionals. Timo is shifting from pastoral care to equipping and mobilizing nonformal disciple makers.

Some leaders in the Berlin coalition have opted to start multiple gospel initiatives led by teams of missionaries and lay volunteers. They believe that movement will be achieved only through a significant increase of evange-lism and discipleship in the marketplaces of life. They have started outreach ministries in common spaces like cafés, where Christians can live out and verbalize their faith as they rub shoulders with Berliners. Others are at-tempting to penetrate immigrant subgroups by helping them adjust to the city. The key is building a pool of disciples who are also disciple makers.

14. The urban church-planting mission started by Redeemer Presbyterian Church in New York City.

As the church in Pankow grew, Timo delegated leadership responsibilities and began coaching other church planters. Two years ago, he started to sense God's call to a broader ministry as a catalyst. He realized he would have to devote more time to gathering others around a church-planting vision for the city. He recruited additional staff and volunteers, so he could give two-thirds of his time to this regional vision.

He was already part of an umbrella network called *Together for Berlin*. He shared his vision with a veteran church-planting leader and together they approached key players from different church groups, finally gathering a group of eight. He now gives only a third of his time to his local church and has more time to work regionally. When asked what helped him develop as a church-planting catalyst, he replied:

1. The culture of developing others, investing in another generation.

2. Learning to invest in others instead of taking charge and doing it himself.

3. Reading that helped him manage *through others* and take steps forward in organizational leadership.

4. Developing skills in coaching, facilitating, gathering others around a vision.

5. Patience waiting for God's timing, rather than forcing growth.

6. Observing a brother who served as a strategic thinker and motivator.

What does Timo do as a catalyst? He visits church plants and coaches their church planters. Some have invited him to help their teams in specific areas of skill or vision. He recently took some of the planters he is coaching to a workshop on movements. He explains that he rarely has the time or resources to create church-planting events himself but enjoys collaborating with others and connecting people with opportunities.

Timo encourages, equips, and empowers others, keenly aware that transforming Berlin with the gospel will take several generations. He sees a need to help the network transition to a more active role implementing the vision in concrete ways and recruiting others for greater capacity. He takes part in catalytic events that mobilize prayer, interest, and investment in the movement for Berlin to Christ. Rather than focusing on the enormity of the task, he is asking people to pray that for an increase in committed Christ-followers from 2 to 3 percent in Berlin.

Timo has not yet seen multiplication take off but has been persistently building a network and mobilizing others to pray to that end. One encouraging sign is that *houses of prayer* are interceding twenty-four hours a day for a movement of God.[15] One of Timo's friends reported that her church recently had a revival week. Members went out into the streets, danced, sang, gave testimonies, prayed for people, and talked about Jesus. Many were moved, some cried, and some were healed. Most amazingly, ninety-five people made professions of faith in three days.

Position and title do not make a church-planting catalyst. Catalysts are more than resource people although they have a ready repertoire of resources. They use coaching but have a broader ministry than that of a coach. They are change agents—activators with movement vision who ignite faith, mobilize people, and channel resources to see that vision become a reality. Part of their ministry flows from their being and gifting, but another part is developed in the harvest field. Believing that God is doing something new and unique when he infuses the gospel into new territory, they see other cultures as expressions of God's creative handiwork and adapt ministry to them.

Facilitating gospel movements requires a shift to paradigms consonant with this kind of indigenous ministry—values like facilitative leadership, relational partnership, cultural adaptation, home grown strategies, discovery learning, kingdom cooperation, and local resourcing. Not all catalysts are successful in making this shift, but many are. The chapter that follows outlines best practices and ministry structures for grassroots church multiplication.

15. Houses of prayer are centers where Christians come together to pray in rotating fashion twenty-four hours a day, or as close to that as they can. Timo feeds missional prayer requests to them.

9

Movement Mindset

Catalysts are quick to affirm that they don't create gospel movements but not as prone to recognize that they can get in the way. Some roadblocks to healthy growth come from the enemy, or from the difficulties of the terrain; but occasionally, movement slows because of something self-inflicted and preventable. Like runners who watch for potholes and shed needless weight, wise catalysts avert distractions and avoid hindrances.

The Facilitator Era not only requires a different type of ministry, but it also calls for a distinct mindset and paradigm shifts. Catalysts help others see old realities through new lenses. New insights remove mental roadblocks and unlock possibilities that were formerly invisible.

The shift to facilitation means redefining success and adopting new metrics. Catalysts no longer focus on personal accomplishments, but rather on the fruitfulness of those they are mentoring and coaching. The best seller, *When Helping Hurts*, provides a pathway to walk constructively with the materially poor instead of providing short-term fixes or creating long-term dependencies.[1]

Likewise, the paradigms in this chapter will help readers contribute wisely to the spiritual and strategic needs of partners, building empowering relationships for years to come. When catalysts have a controlling mindset, they soon get into trouble; but when they go to listen, learn, and complement, they add value to what God is already doing. Many are not willing or

---

1. Corbett and Fikkert, *When Helping Hurts*, 99–185.

able to shift to a facilitative posture. They want to be the permanent pillars, rather than temporary scaffolding.

We will look at seven core values that undergird the *empowering of indigenous multiplication ministry* (see figure 9.1).

Figure 9.1. *Paradigms That Support Indigenous Multiplication Ministry*

REASONS FOR INDIGENOUS MINISTRY

There is a theological reason to make this shift, no matter how we feel about it. The body of Christ within each people group has the primary responsibility to reach and disciple their people. They are also best equipped to communicate the gospel and give ministries culturally relevant forms, which are also reproducible. Therefore, local churches are called to become self-propagating, self-leading, and self-supporting as soon as possible. People from other cultures may have to lay a foundation, and expatriates can and should help, but they should not take over and call the shots.

Following the lead of Rufus Anderson and Henry Venn, John Nevius advocated these three *self-principles* in a series of articles in the Chinese

Recorder journal in 1885, which was later published as a book in 1886 entitled *The Planting and Development of Missionary Churches*.[2] These principles of indigenous ministry were revolutionary when John Nevius and others first started to apply them, but today we recognize them as fundamental to gospel movements.

Gospel movements are indigenous. They draw upon homegrown leadership and resources and use local forms because "if the church is to be indigenous it must spring up in the soil from the very first seeds planted."[3] External catalysts should always facilitate and protect indigeneity, holding their models and preferences lightly and using external resources cautiously. Too often time and resources are squandered, and major mistakes made, because catalysts have thought that they knew best.

An indigenous gospel movement began in the wake of the 2004 tsunami that rocked northern Sumatra, a Muslim-majority island of Indonesia. An Indonesian mission sent eight teams to work with three people groups. Five teams were assigned to the Acehnese, the most resistant group, and three were assigned to Malay groups (the Mandailing and Malay Deli people). These teams were collectively composed of eighteen Indonesian families and one single person, mostly Bible school graduates from other Indonesian tribes.

As expected, the work among the Acehnese progressed slowly as a foundation of trust was being laid. All three teams working among the Malay have been fruitful, but only one has experienced multiplication. The church planted by that team experienced four generations of reproduction from 2008 to 2016. As of December 2016, sixteen house churches were meeting regularly among the Malay Deli people! Seven of them were first-generation, four were second-generation, two were third-generation, and three were fourth-generation house churches.

Surprisingly, local teams affirmed the growth was not due to greater receptivity among the Malay Deli. The field workers we interviewed affirmed that the critical factor was the *shift to indigenous ministry* that took place when local believers were equipped and empowered to share the gospel, make disciples, and lead churches. A person close to the situation explained, "Since the witnesses are local, they are more easily accepted by local people. All house churches are among Malay Deli people. Each house church is led by locals." What led to this breakthrough?

The year 2014 was a turning point. After attending a T4T training, one of the Indonesian missionaries shifted the focus to preparing

2. Weber, *Layman*, 350.
3. Allen, *Spontaneous Expansion*, 2.

Muslim-background local leaders. Soon afterward, he turned over all visible leadership to local leaders. He stood behind them and mentored them while giving them the authority to lead house churches. Now, in this region, the local leaders lead the churches and ministries. They do not receive salaries, only occasional help in times of need. They pray for people, share the gospel, make disciples, and equip members of the house church to do the same. It has become a grassroots disciple-making movement.

Too often, outsiders stay in the driver's seat much too long. In most cases, they should never take the steering wheel, but help local leaders from the passenger seat. Local Christians will make mistakes; some may falter, but gospel movements must ultimately be led by them. Now we turn to the supporting paradigms that enhance catalytic ministry and the dangers that come from ignoring them.

PARADIGMS IN SUPPORT OF INDIGENOUS MULTIPLICATION MINISTRY

Cultural Adaptation

A one-shot, parachute approach will not do. Time is needed to build relationships and understand culture. Many catalysts are gifted teachers; but to be effective internationally or in multicultural cities they need much more. Effective catalysts are other-focused and culturally aware. They take time to observe and listen before acting and adjust to the realities on the ground. They learn to grasp the mental maps of those they are serving and help them with new narratives when culture stands against the gospel. They seek wisdom to discern the motivation of potential partners, cultural intelligence to avoid misunderstandings, and situational awareness to respond appropriately to surprises.

They go slowly at first, ask a lot of questions, and get counsel from cultural insiders. Knowing the origins and history of the people will help. Who were the gospel movement founders and what was their early vision? How did the movement grow? Mapping church plants, streams of discipleship, and generations of reproduction will reveal patterns and changes needed (see Life Center case study at the end of chap. 2).

In oral cultures, new ideas are transmitted through story and song. Narratives and modeling are used to introduce unfamiliar concepts because didactic instruction alone rarely leads to lasting change. Several members of our team of catalysts discovered this the hard way. They traveled to northern Thailand to train leaders from the Lahu people, a tribal group that had earlier experienced a PMC movement. The young pastors and Bible school students faithfully took notes and participated in discussions. Although the principles were well received, they were not generally applied because the Lahu are oral learners. They need stories, demonstration, and repetition to bring truth to life. Introducing an abstract concept is not sufficient; these concrete learners need real life examples.

The Lahu also process change differently, and slowly. They want to discuss with their elders, build consensus, and work together. Individual initiative, applauded in the West, is suspect among them. When one of the Lahu partners succeeded in transitioning to multiplication ministry, others began taking note and change is beginning to take place.

Home Grown Strategies

External catalysts must distinguish between transferable principles, fruitful practices, and contextual strategies. Transferable principles are rooted in Scripture and apply broadly. They are nonnegotiables that must be fleshed out in each context. For example, every church should be a disciple-making community. This is a transferable principle, but how it is fleshed out will vary.

Fruitful practices are patterns or approaches that have been found to be effective within people that share a common culture. Finding a person of peace who is open to learning about Jesus is a gateway to the community in middle eastern cities and Hindu villages. Likewise, ministry to physical and educational needs has opened doors among Syrian refugees. Finding prepared people is a best practice, but seekers look different depending on the culture.

Finally, contextual strategies are the tactics that flow from the principles and fruitful practices. Discovery Bible Studies (DBS) have been widely used, with good results, among the displaced Syrians in Lebanon and many others. However, DBS is not the best approach in all situations. Recorded Bible stories work well in rural Tajikistan, while written texts or Internet messages may be more effective among Tajik students in the capital.

Some succumb to the danger of becoming rigid in their strategies, uncritically applying a methodology that worked elsewhere. They insist that all workers use their programs and strategies exclusively. They do so to their own detriment. These things are only channels and tools. Methods should be homegrown or tested rather than transplanted uncritically.

The person God used to start the greatest documented CPM asked at a conference (in my presence) why his methodology, so successful in China, did not seem to be working in the United States. He replied that those who had tried to use his approach had not been faithful to it. To use a cooking metaphor, the cake did not rise because they had not followed the recipe carefully enough. Trousdale and Sunshine use the same analogy: "Keep in mind, the approach we outline here is like a recipe: it doesn't work without all the ingredients in place."[4]

Methods and tactics should not be formulaic, like recipe books, but should always take the local situation into account. Wise catalysts will test them rather than use them as rubber stamps. Methodological flexibility and adaptability to local context are critical components of indigenous ministry.

Relational Partnership

Contextualization is facilitated by solid partnerships. Effective catalysts are willing to invest in fraternal relationships that encourage and empower. Those relationships are not just a means to an end; they are a gift and a pathway to fruitfulness. They must be real, cultivated intentionally, nurtured with humility and respect, and built on shared values that transcend culture. Catalysts who value indigenous ministry view national partners as equals and seek to learn from them. If you see a long-term partnership that has produced fruit for the gospel, you will often find, at its core, this kind of mutually edifying relationship.

External catalysts who work in multiple settings for short periods of time are in danger of having a *parachutist* mentality. Parachutists are welcome in time of crisis or combat where rapid deployment is needed. However, the parachutist mentality does not serve gospel movements well. Expert consultants, visiting professors, and teaching pastors may contribute something positive, but to have a lasting impact they must learn the culture and build relationships. That usually takes time, follow-up calls, and return visits.

Our team members have learned to plan extra time before and after equipping events to meet with leaders, their teams, and families. Debriefing afterward around a shared meal can provide valuable insights. Often, shared trials become the instruments God uses to forge and grow friendships. Sickness, cultural challenges, spiritual conflict, and other forms of adversity can bring partners into a deeper level of trust. Yet, relationships are insufficient in themselves: Indigenous ministry calls for a different leadership stance on the part of catalysts.

---

4. Trousdale and Sunshine, *Kingdom Unleashed*, 406.

Facilitative Leadership

Although the primary ministry of catalysts is to develop and empower others, they still have a leadership function. They are change agents, but they go about it differently than local church leaders. They build on what is already there. "Rather than initiate, facilitators enhance. Rather than do the job, they aid and champion its completion."[5] Catalysts facilitate change by mobilizing, gathering, equipping, empowering, and assisting. A mobilizer describes this catalytic leadership function as a pathway toward multiplication:

> The nature of this new era hinges on today's mission leaders and missionaries becoming proficient as catalytic leaders. In the past, missionaries needed to be pioneers or strategists to do the work for the church. But today—with unprecedented connectedness—missionaries also need to be catalytic leaders to empower every disciple to play a part. They must learn to act as a conduit toward exponential missions impact.[6]

Some talk about unleashing or releasing national partners. The truth is that facilitative leaders should never have to release what they never owned or controlled. The temptation to control is a real danger. Catalysts, in their desire to see people come into line with the vision, will be tempted to make things happen themselves, in their own power. Only mutual learning and empowerment can provide true partnership in the Facilitator Era. This applies to all areas—finances, education, and strategic planning. Facilitative leaders can receive as well as give, learn as well as teach, and follow as well as lead.

Discovery Learning

Dave Hunt, former president of *City Teams*, analyzed the results of a co-operative five-year partnership between their mission and an indigenous organization in East Africa. He found that over four thousand churches had been started in countries that had been resistant to the gospel. Many factors contributed to the multiplication of disciples and churches. But none of it would have been possible with the old traditional models. New ways of seeing and doing were needed.

> From the beginning of this church multiplication project, it was clear that there needed to be a new way of doing church. Rapid

5. Steffen, *Facilitator Era*, 63–64.
6. Davis, "New Era of Modern Mission," para. 14.

multiplication of churches, a real movement, would not happen using the existing forms of church. It would not be possible to generate enough money, sufficient professional leaders, or adequate management systems to expand the current model to the point of covering every city, village, community, and neighborhood in the region.[7]

Hunt led a group of leaders through a reexamination of what it means to be a disciple and what *church* really is, according to the original text. The source of discovery was Scripture itself. Once the essence of *church* was captured, the peripherals, cultural preferences, and extrabiblical traditions were recognized for what they were—stumbling blocks. The discovery approach helped church leaders embrace new wineskins and pass them on to those in their sphere of influence, using the same discovery approach.

Discovery learning is not only needed in the Horn of Africa. We have found that, wherever cultural Christianity has developed traditional ways of looking at things and doing things, a fresh look at the *Source* is warranted. In the Czech Republic, the president of the Czech Brethren association, listening in on a workshop about reproducing disciples, commented: "This is great teaching, but I recommend you focus on the younger generation." He was warning us that some people are so entrenched in their thinking that they could not adopt new patterns, even if they agreed and wanted to. Understanding the challenge of worldview change, he recommended starting with a new generation of church planters.

Local Resourcing

Resources are most appreciated and effective when they are available at the point of need. The timely access to resources can be a game changer. But catalysts should not rush to alleviate hardship and meet needs. Wise ones avoid becoming the providers and problem-solvers. Instead, they ask questions to help others discover the untapped assets around them. On the other hand, they dare not remain cold hearted and unresponsive. They often can help workers find local materials, make connections, do research, attend training, or receive counseling. Sometimes they will contribute a resource directly. But they will rarely become the primary resource themselves.

A related danger is the resource-driven ministry. Sadly, some well-funded catalysts, wanting to get things done, offer to pay national workers to run their programs. In places like Haiti and Mongolia, some of the most gifted pastors and church planters have left their ministries to take

7. Hunt, "Revolution in Church Multiplication," 77–78.

paid positions in nonprofits. While the recruiting of church leaders for parachurch ministries may be legitimate at times, the leadership vacuum it creates in churches and emerging movements is sometimes harmful and happens with alarming frequency.

Facilitating and enabling are two different things. Enabling puts the catalyst, not the local disciple, in the driver's seat. Over the long term, it leads to ministries that are not relevant, sustainable, or reproducible.[8] The primary guideline is that, whether applied to a local church or a movement of churches, local ministries should be supported locally as soon as possible and as much as possible. Fixed, recurring expenses should be covered by local believers. Generosity is always a virtue, but it can undermine growth when it becomes a substitute for local stewardship and responsibility. Infusions of outside aid are welcomed in times of special need or for one-time projects. Outside investment is most fruitful when used to equip local people with the income-generating skills they need to support their ministry.

Kingdom Cooperation

Catalysts can function like lone rangers instead of team players. This is counterproductive in the long run for two reasons. First, we do not want to see just any kind of churches planted, but long to see a movement of healthy, reproducing ones that make disciples and transform their social environments. This requires a spectrum of biblical instruction—family health, spiritual disciplines, biblical leadership, teaching principles, church planting, pastoral ministry, to name a few. And for that to happen, wise cooperation among catalysts and trainers is needed. The developmental needs of the movement must be discerned through prayer, assessment, and dialogue with national partners. Then a plan can be designed to bring in different catalysts in appropriate sequence, according to the stage and growth needs of the movement.

Secondly, if catalysts want to foster healthy collaboration *within* gospel movements, they too should model it by working as a team. Too often international agencies have promoted unity but practiced competition, or just turned a blind eye to what others are doing. Kingdom cooperation among catalysts contributes to healthy indigenous ministry.

Commitment to indigenous ministry is needed. Otherwise, it would be easy to slide into harmful, self-centered patterns of thinking and acting. These paradigm shifts toward indigeneity will not, in and of themselves,

8. For a more thorough discussion of the constructive use of finances in movements, see chap. 18 of *Global Church Planting* (Ott and Wilson, 2011).

lead to multiplication, but they will get stagnated movements off foreign life support and free new ones to grow without external restraints.

The story of ReachAfrica illustrates how church leaders with missionary vision can create empowering structures and share resources to transform entire countries. The driving force came from their passion for unreached people groups. Seven men stayed up all night wrestling with the question, "What can we do to evangelize the millions of unreached people of Africa?"

THE REACHAFRICA STORY

In April 2007, a group of American missionaries serving in Africa met in Nairobi, Kenya, with leaders from several African movements for training, encouragement, and ministry connections. However, God had bigger purposes in mind. During that time, the former executive director of Reach-Global mission expressed the vision to influence more than one hundred million people for Christ in ten years. The Lord began to lay on the hearts of the African church leaders their responsibility toward the unreached in Africa. Seven of them stayed up all night praying, singing, and asking God what to do about the millions in Africa who did not have the gospel. Rev. Nubako Selenga, one of the men who was present, explains:

> God was giving us a great desire and burden in the heart of African leaders who were there to reach the unreached in Africa by the power of the Good News of Jesus Christ. We started to understand that this was really our responsibility for Africa. After sharing what God was laying on our hearts during the conference, the ReachGlobal leaders surrounded us and prayed for us.[9]

The group of seven heard and courageously accepted God's call to raise up a new generation of African church-planting missionaries. Then they gathered a couple more times within the next year to form a coalition they called ReachAfrica and formulate a missionary strategy. They established a clear mission statement, identified shared ministry values, and set up a simple organizational structure. They chose Nubako Selenga, former president of the Evangelical Free Church of the Democratic Republic of Congo, as president and David Kiamu from Liberia as church planting director.

In May 2009, Selenga and Kiamu attended the *Exponential Conference* in Orlando, Florida, along with ReachGlobal Africa area leader Kevin

---

9. Selenga, "ReachAfrica Report."

Kompelien. Craig Ott from Trinity Evangelical Divinity School and I helped them design an equipping plan that could accelerate healthy apostolic church planting and prepare church-planting missionaries without formal theological education.

Later that year, Selenga and Kiamu made exploratory visits to Mali, Ivory Coast, and Niger, countries with many unreached people groups. They also launched Church Multiplication Training (CMT) in Togo to mobilize and equip national church planters. The following year, they offered the same church planter training in Monrovia, Liberia. Soon the missions effort extended into neighboring Ivory Coast as well. Civil war broke out there in 2010, as it had in Liberia a decade earlier. Titus Davis (chap. 6) led a team to the border of Ivory Coast, taking the gospel, along with bags of rice and bundles of clothing. They ministered to hundreds of refugees in camps. They also found a *household of peace* in Gbinta, inside the Ivory Coast. Titus explains: "We presented the gospel and they believed and accepted our Lord Jesus as Savior. We prayed for them and challenged them to keep the faith. They agreed to be our contact in Ivory Coast. As a church planter, I am thinking of launching a CPM starting with this family."[10]

By 2011, 208 church planters from four countries had received the basic training, and Selenga and Kiamu adopted the goal of equipping one thousand church planters and one hundred master trainers. Soon, existing churches were starting daughters, and new churches were being birthed among the poor, broken, and destitute. Church planting accelerated. So did the need for guidance to grow biblically sound and spiritually healthy churches. Mark Wold, a Californian who had revitalized several struggling US churches, and Kiamu of ReachAfrica developed a curriculum to teach principles of church health.

Their core belief was that only transformed lives can transform others. Gospel transformation requires that church leaders and disciples emphasize worldview change and life renewal from the inside out. That calls for the breaking of old spiritual bonds and falsehoods through the Word and Spirit. Zambian trainer Edward Mwanza took both CMT and Church Health Training (CHT) to Malawi, Zimbabwe, Namibia, Angola, Tanzania, and Kenya.

In February 2012, leaders who had received and implemented CMT gathered to learn how to function as regional master trainers in two regional centers: Monrovia, Liberia; and Kinshasa, Democratic Republic of the Congo. The curriculum was developed by Selenga and Kiamu who produced a manual and a process to equip master trainers. Every church

10. Davis, "Evangelical Free Church of West Africa Report."

planter was empowered to reproduce the training under the oversight and coordination of a master trainer. The ReachAfrica leaders and master trainers formed a visionary coalition of volunteers to multiply disciple-making churches throughout Africa.

This network of master trainers has been a critical factor in the expansion of ReachAfrica. Since funds for living expenses, travel, and training were limited, they had to own the cause and mobilize the resources in their respective regions. In November 2012, Abraham Mudidi, one of the master trainers, was sent from Kinshasa to Kitwe, Zambia to do level-one CMT. Some of the leaders in Kitwe reproduced the training in Botswana and South Africa. Like a spreading grapevine, the ministry was introduced in neighboring countries through preexisting relationships and networks.

The training itself has been reproduced in French, Portuguese, Amharic, and Swahili. Since 2007, the equipping ministry of ReachAfrica has spread to thirteen of the fifteen countries in West Africa and has impacted a total of thirty-two African countries.[11] In 2018, the ReachAfrica leaders designed a plan around the vision of equipping fifty thousand church planters to launch disciple-making churches among a hundred unreached and unengaged people groups, primarily in sub-Saharan Islamic countries, by equipping African churches for pioneer church planting in difficult places.

The story of ReachAfrica is ongoing. Its leaders are finding that, although support structures do not make the movement, they become necessary when it reaches the stages of regional organization and global participation. Structures like training, missional partnerships, and church-planting networks enabled an organization with few financial resources to grow along relational lines and impact an entire continent. Passion for the lost, gospel zeal, and fervent prayer were the engine behind these African movements and ReachAfrica's leadership and equipping structure provided tracks on which they traveled.

We have looked at several dimensions of the ministry of church-planting catalysts—their major roles, their character and qualities, and the values that shape their efforts. In the chapter that follows we ask the questions, "What is the role of organization, and what structures will strengthen, accelerate, and extend the reach of gospel movements?" Catalytic ministry can be compared to a vehicle with four wheels: assessing, coaching, mobilizing, and equipping. The wheels do not run the car, but if one of them is missing, or deflated, the ride will be bumpy and will most likely be cut short.

11. Dalrymple, "ReachGlobal Report—Africa Division."

10

Support Structures for Healthy Movements

The need for church-planting catalysts is increasingly recognized in Western denominations. Baptists, Methodists, and many others have regional catalysts. Sometimes a catalyst's ministry description is prescribed by a mission organization whose systems are already in place. Strategy coordinators for the IMB (Southern Baptists) were early catalysts for CPMs. Today T4T, DMM, and other multiplication ministries, all have their version of catalysts.

God is also raising up catalysts within emerging movements in the Global South. Word of Life, the largest Evangelical denomination in Ethiopia, already had one in place when we first visited Addis Ababa. In April 2014, two missionaries serving in Africa offered level-one CMT to about twenty-five local leaders representing several denominations. The Ethiopian Catalyst, Alemayehu (Alex) recognized two problems: The manual needed to be rewritten for Ethiopia, and the participants were not practitioners who could apply and reproduce the training. Alex decided to fill in the gap. He adapted the content and translated it into Amharic. Then he made a list of influential church planters who would train others.

In October of that year, he repeated the training three times with experienced church planters whom he selected personally. They reproduced it in their regions, so that in less than a year, 458 people received the training, and fifty-five new churches were started. In all, by December 2014, CMT had been reproduced three or four times by passionate church-planting leaders. Why was this equipping partnership more fruitful than many others?

When we arrived, the table was already set. The commitment to reach the lost and make disciples was already there. Someone invested in Alex, and he poured his life in others. A passionate and competent reproducer was in place with an established equipping network. As a cultural insider, he had already won the trust of other evangelical groups. The ministry patterns and support systems he developed are serving to accelerate gospel movements in many other places.

THE NEED FOR SUPPORT SYSTEMS AND STRUCTURES

A system is a set of interacting or interdependent components, forming an integrated whole, that supports a human endeavor.[1] Structures under gird those systems. Some argue that talk of systems and structures sounds like imposing a business model on church growth. Others object that structures become limiting and lead to movement paralysis. Also, some CPM advocates do not recognize the stages that gospel movements go through and argue for minimal structure and uniform strategy throughout the life of the movement. They tend to downplay the need for levels of leadership, theological education, and organization.

These fears are understandable and can be legitimate. We have found that organizational structure can be premature, excessive, or inappropriate. But although structure imposed from the outside can hurt movement, aversion to all and any structure can be a dangerous over-reaction. Stage-appropriate, homegrown structures that provide for coordinated effort can strengthen and extend movements. Why bother with support systems?

First, systems are needed for healthy growth. Structure originally was created by God to sustain life and health in the biological sphere. Think of the skeletal system, the circulatory system, or digestive system of our bodies. Or consider the ecological system at work in nature: Thousands of living things are sustained through an interlocking network that produces nutrients and provides conditions necessary for survival. Those systems were designed by the Creator. What do they have in common? They work together to sustain life and growth. Likewise, in ministry, wise leaders create timely structures that facilitate progress, without exceeding what is needed.

Secondly, although they are not mandated, we find biblical precedent for support structures. God started the first gospel movement from Jerusalem without any preestablished formal structures. But as *the Way* grew,

---

1. The word "system" from the Greek *sustēma* comes from *sun* ("with") and *histanai* ("set up"). Thus, systems can refer to things used to set up or support our work.

the apostles and Jerusalem elders determined under the Spirit's guidance how best to choose deacons, establish elders, send missionaries, and solve conflicts threatening to divide the church. They gathered for church councils and sent out official emissaries. Structure grew with the movement to address needs.

Thirdly, support structures allow leaders to be good stewards of their limited resources. Growth brings increased demands and complexity. Wise leaders can create pathways to navigate those complexities, and structures to carry the weight.

> Systems enable us to do things over and over again, expending less energy because we have created a process. They help us think about the best ways to do things and to continually improve what we do . . . We use systems in all of life to create efficiencies, become more productive, maintain quality, and evaluate to improve our work. They are a tool that can be used for good or evil.[2]

Finally, we should ask: "What would happen to a movement if no structure existed?" The movement will be unmanageable and eventually flounder if it relies solely on the giftedness and passion of its founders. At some point, movement pioneers reach the limit of their reproductive capacity. Without other gifted people, resources, and structures, growth becomes unsustainable, and the movement will stall or splinter. As gospel movements grow, structure facilitates local multiplication, regional organization, and global participation. Structures that are premature, inappropriate, or excessive weigh a movement down, but timely and nimble support systems facilitate growth. They are friends of gospel movements like the trellis is a friend to the grapevine (see figure 10.1).

Figure 10.1. *The Trellis Supports Healthy Growth*

2. Pinney, "Catalyzing Movements," 7–8.

A trellis is a framework of light wooden or metal bars, chiefly used as a support for fruit trees or climbing plants. The trellis enhances the grapevine's health. It doesn't produce growth, but facilitates it by putting the vine, and its clusters of grapes, in the best possible position to receive what they need to grow and bear fruit. The uprights hold up the branches, exposing their fruit to the sunlight. They keep the foliage off the ground and away from insects. In the end, the trellis improves the quality of the grapes and increases the productivity of the vine.

No one gets excited about the trellis; its value is in the function it serves. Likewise, church-planting support systems, provided they are indigenous and appropriate, not only strengthen movements, but also accelerate their fruitfulness and extend their lifespan so that they reach maturity and give birth to new movements.

Leadership development is a good example. John L. Nevius had seen the damage created when missionaries controlled the churches in China. Forced to leave China, he went to Korea and, in 1889, helped to prepare the new team of missionaries there. The two weeks of instruction he gave them provided form and focus to their work. He taught that churches should be shaped by local culture, led by local leaders, and supported by local funds. He developed a plan to prepare workers and train them in the Word.

The Korea mission considered the *Nevius Plan* so important that they adopted it as mission policy and gave all new missionaries a copy of his booklet, requiring them to pass an examination on it. This training structure facilitated the amazing Korean gospel movement described in chapter 2. Pierard, a professor of history at Indiana State University, gives Nevius's four criteria for deploying local leaders:

- Each Christian should support himself by his own work and be a witness for Christ by life and word in his own neighborhood.

- Church methods and structures should be developed only as far as the indigenous Christians could take responsibility for these.

- Local churches should select for full-time work those who seem best qualified and whom they are able to support.

- Church buildings were to be built in local style and by the Christians from their own resources.[3]

At the time, new believers were often taken from their families, usually for their own protection, and expected to live on missionary compounds or bases. From there they went on forays into town and villages, under

3. Pierard, "John Livingston Nevius," 700.

the direction of foreign missionaries. Nevius's system of preparing workers facilitated the transition from this colonial approach to the indigenous approach of releasing them immediately to witness and equipping them progressively as they served Christ in their communities.

The most recognized church-planting support systems are summed up in the acronym ABCD: Assessment, Basic Training, Coaching, and Development. "The ABCDs of church planting are really the creation of systems which enable us to plant more churches, better churches, and multiply workers for the harvest!"[4]

A—*Assessment* helps to select the workers with the right profile and gifts.

B—*Basic Training* brings key biblical principles and best practices to them.

C—*Coaching* helps to implement those concepts and overcome obstacles on the way.

D—*Development* supports workers in their efforts, so they can grow and persevere.

These support structures, like a skeleton, give stability and strength. They also grow with the organism rather than starting out full-sized, waiting for the flesh, muscle, and other organs to catch up!

THE PRIMARY FUNCTIONS OF CATALYSTS

The goal of catalysts is to add value to what God is already doing. Both task and context should be considered when deciding how to engage as a catalyst. Part of it is intuitive, flowing from giftedness, understanding, and care for church planters and their work, but most of it is learned by observing others. Catalysts have at least four primary functions that answer four fundamental questions.

Where Will We Find People and Resources? (Mobilizing Function)

Catalysts cast vision and highlight opportunities to mobilize people and resources for gospel movement. They gather people around a significant vision that requires kingdom cooperation. Steffen describes the synergy needed: "Pioneers conceptualize a church-planting movement and find the personnel, expats, and nationals to make it happen. Facilitators visualize

4. Pinney, "Catalyzing Movements," 8.

the big picture and know which people and organizations, when brought together, can implement the vision."[5]

Early on, catalysts identify or develop a church-planting network that will organize and give oversight to church-planting efforts. Then they work with and through the local network to move toward multiplication through mobilizing activity such as:

- Gathering people to make strategies and develop an action plan.

- Working with local people to identify local resources to achieve the plan.

- Sharing the vision and helping others start similar networks.

- Finding champions and church-planting visionaries to expand the work.

David Kiamu (chap. 6) brought together five distinct associations to strategize and equip church planters to reach the least evangelized regions of Liberia. This was the beginning of a coalition that impacted nine West African countries during his ministry. In each country, he worked with a church-planting champion who developed their church-planting network. He coached the network champion who organized training events and gathered funds for them. The champion worked with a master trainer to equip workers. Others were recruited for specific areas like prayer and financial support. This simple structure became a railroad track for ReachAfrica's church multiplication expansion.

Who Can Effectively Reproduce Disciples and Plant Churches? (Assessing Function)

Catalysts help their local partners develop a process to select those who will be most effective as church planters. The best evaluation is done by observing potential church planters in action. Selection is enhanced by interviewing them and others who know them well, using past behavior as a predictor of potential. Prior fruitfulness carries more weight in the assessment process than knowledge or good intentions.

Assessment criteria are developed by studying what makes a church planter effective *in that context*. The list of competencies becomes the basis for creating a planter profile used for assessment. There is a common core referred to as the 4 C's: Character, Competency, Conjugal Support,

---

5. Steffen, *Facilitator Era*, 61.

and Compatibility (sometimes called chemistry). Competency includes the spiritual gifts and skills needed for effective planting in that setting.

Experienced catalysts also learn to evaluate areas of strength and weakness of the movement. Rather than relying on personal judgments, they bring together local leaders to examine the movement based on health and growth indicators.[6] From there they identify problems and obstacles to church growth and reproduction.

How Should Church Planters Be Prepared? (Equipping Function)

"Catalytic movements come as a result of training others."[7] Catalysts tenaciously pray and work toward the multiplication of disciples and churches. They not only point in the right direction—they show the way and model the vision. Whether the need is assessing, training, coaching, consulting, or mobilizing, they invest in people who will contribute to movement growth.

The effective equipping of church planters is an intentional *process* that develops knowledge, attitudes, skills, and character. The last two, skills and character, will often require an apprenticeship or internship that offers on-the-job experience. In oral cultures, apprenticeships (emphasizing modeling and repetition with feedback) should be the primary means of equipping.

Equipping models that are locally relevant, reproducible, and sustainable produce lasting fruit. Both task and context should be considered when deciding on how to prepare someone for a particular ministry. Training can be formal (a course), informal (a coaching relationship), or nonformal (a conference or workshop). These forms of training can be combined for a greater collective impact. We learned from the experience of *Alliance of Saturation Church Planting*, that training must be part of a disciple-making movement and that those invited to training should be planting or ready to start.[8]

What Support Will Planters Need? (Coaching Function)

Catalysts support church planters and help them grow by visiting them, encouraging them, and guiding them in an empowering way. Coaching usually

6. These include David Garrison's ten universal elements of CPMs (2004) and the four stages of movement maturity (Ott, 2017).

7. Miller, "Role of Outsider," 17.

8. Behar, "Reflection," 2.

follows basic training and is most needed when church planters are getting started or entering a new phase. Good coaches ask great questions, helping leaders think for themselves, make wise choices, and grow as people.

When we offered our first coaching clinic in Latin America (chap. 1), we discovered that coaching provided a new model of leadership. Leaders have traditionally used power distance to elevate their status, exert influence, and get things done. Too often, potential leaders have been held at arm's length or treated as assistants to be managed, rather than people to be developed. Those who participated in our coaching clinic did not have a functional substitute for the prevailing cultural leadership model (caudillo or strongman). To our delight, coaching provided one—a coach who comes alongside to develop others. Coaching provided a pathway to raise up a new generation of leaders.

George began his missionary career as a church-planting team member in Montreal, Quebec—the French-speaking province of Canada. In the early 2000s, he realized that for Quebec to be transformed by Christ, French Canadians would have to lead the church-planting charge. Friends from the United States helped him conduct the first of several Church Planter Boot Camps (a four-day workshop to help church planters plan their ministry launch).

Over time, it became clear that a brief event did not adequately prepare bi-vocational church planters for urban church planting in a multicultural context like Montreal. Nothing short of a homegrown equipping system would do. George, having studied civil engineering at the University of Illinois, had a great mind for systems and was always asking, "Is there a better way?" The story that follows shows what God can do through a catalyst who is a systems-thinker and understands the realities of the local context.

CHURCH PLANTING CATALYST
IN QUEBEC, CANADA

George came to Christ through the witness of a friend who later discipled him. Then he got involved in the *Navigators* on campus and learned how to mentor others. He was impacted by Dawson Trotman's saying: "Never do anything that someone else can and will do, when there is so much of importance to be done which others cannot or will not do."[9]

In that spirit, he took on the challenge of working with youth in a large church in the Chicago area and later decided to serve overseas as a missionary. When he found out that Québécois (Quebec's French Canadians) were

9. Quoted in Reynolds, "Dawson Trotman's Personal Spiritual Disciplines," 31.

one of the least reached people groups, not only in the Americas but in the world, he joined a church-planting team headed for Quebec. George and his wife embraced the challenge of learning French and finding their way through the maze of cultures in Montreal. With separatist sentiments running high, Québécois bristled at the evangelistic efforts of neighbors from the south. The high rate of mobility, the blasé attitude of nominal Christians, and the hard winters, all took their toll, but the team persevered.

Part of their vision was to plant churches *with and through* national workers. They invested in others, and several of those they developed went into Christian ministry. One became a teacher in a Quebec Bible school; another returned to France to serve as a church planter; and a third taught philosophy as he developed a new church. Although the team's initial church-planting vision did not work out as they had hoped, local disciples in whom they invested continue to change the spiritual landscape of the province today.

George is a good developer and leader. His contributions were recognized on a regional level. In time, he provided leadership in several church-planting networks, including the Quebec branch of *Church Planting Canada* and *C2C Collective* (Church Planting from Sea to Sea).

The denomination in which he was involved also asked him to help them mobilize church planting. The group had grown significantly in the 1980s and 1990s but had plateaued and lost some of its church-planting fervor. George believed that to be successful, they would have to develop teams of bi-vocational church planters and equip them in cohorts to plant churches. The design he created combines nonformal and informal education with practical experience.

In 2015, he launched, along with others, an equipping process for bi-vocational church planters for called CRAIE—"chalk" in French—an acronym meaning *Regional Church Planting Learning Community* to develop and support teams of lay planters for Quebec's cities. More of a process than program, CRAIE incorporates on-the-job experience with self-study, learning community, classroom, and coaching. This integrated approach has two selling points: People do not have to leave their jobs to be part of a church-planting ministry, and they can learn and work in teams.

Participants invest twenty Saturdays over a two-year period, do 240 hours of reading and homework, and receive twenty hours of coaching per year, while they serve on a church-planting team. George led an equipping team that taught and coached participants while they planted churches, and his wife coached some of the women.

In 2017, nineteen people signed up, forming two cohorts. They worked, directly or indirectly, in four different church plants. Since participants apply as they learn, the work-study serves as a testing ground as well. Participants discover their strengths and deficiencies and develop a clearer sense of their gifting and calling. As a result, some continue church planting afterward while others decide to work in existing churches or parachurch work.

In 2019, George passed the leadership baton to Jonathan, a young Québécois that he had mentored over the years. He continues to work as a regional catalyst in Quebec while he serves internationally to facilitate gospel movements in North India, Thailand, and Myanmar. His ministry in Montreal has given him the understanding and credibility to serve globally. His passion is to develop national catalysts who will continue when he is gone.

After doing several levels of training in North India, George is better able to spot apostolic leaders and come alongside them. Most often they are not the positional leaders within the movements, but rather field leaders working in the harvest. Arjun is a case in point. He came uninvited to the Church Planting Catalyzer training when someone else could not make it. He soaked in the content, went back home, and shared the vision of multiplying churches. They decided to establish four training centers. Another cross-cultural catalyst coached Arjun after the event.

When George returned to North India the following year, Arjun had gathered thirty-five potential regional multipliers. George and Arjun worked with them for the better part of a day. Then these leaders joined one hundred and twenty-five local pastors and potential church planters for two days of training emphasizing reproducing disciples. George reported in a ministry report, "Arjun and his wife ended up attending the June training *by accident*. They took the principles home and completely redirected their ministry due to the training, producing amazing results!"[10]

This breakthrough illustrates the Spirit-led synergy that is possible when external catalysts join forces with local leaders. To sustain movement, these men are investing in another generation of reproducers. Their work will be strengthened by using simple support structures like assessment, basic training, coaching, and development. Our deep desire in sharing these examples and principles is to provide a pathway for catalysts to:

- understand the spiritual dynamics, indigenous nature, stages, and discipling core of gospel movements;

- assess the stage of maturity of a gospel movement and engage with appropriate interventions and resources;

- take the posture of a catalyst (facilitator) and develop and empower movement leaders in appropriate ways;

10. Pinney, "Eternal Perspectives," 1.

- grow in key roles and develop best practices to be effective in catalytic ministry;

- identify and develop the personal qualities needed to be a fruitful catalyst;

- select other catalysts in which to invest.

George did not transition to a facilitative regional ministry overnight. He loved being a church-planting pastor and was gifted in that role. But one day it became clear to his supervisors and to him that he should turn church leadership over to local men and women even though they might not be fully prepared. Because he made that transition, George is helping dozens of church planters in Quebec and Asia. Shifting to a catalytic ministry may sound challenging. It requires conviction and intentionality. After looking under the hood of gospel movements in the New Testament and several eras of church history, including our own, we conclude with this important question, "Where do we go from here?"

11

Where Do We Go from Here?

In the foreword of this book, Steve Addison paints a thrilling picture of the advance of gospel movements in the Global South. These are exciting days. The church is growing twice as fast as the population in much of Africa. In Asia UPGs are being seeded with simple churches by the thousands. In some Central and Latin America countries the percentage of Evangelical Christians now equals or exceeds that of the United States. Among the top ten missionary-sending nations we now find countries like Brazil, South Korea, India, Nigeria, and the Philippines. Former mission fields are now part of God's new mission force.

There are also some areas of concern. The missionary enterprise had been "the West to the rest," but now the percentage of Christians in Western nations no longer keeps up with the population growth and Europe and North America are receiving missionaries. Many historic movements have plateaued or are declining. Their church leaders are looking at the explosive growth of indigenous movements and wondering: "What is behind those dynamic movements, and can we capture some of it?" Reactions are mixed, adding to existing tensions about the church's mission and priorities. In some circles, positions have hardened between advocates and opponents of CPM strategies.

Where there is confusion and uncertainty, it is always good to go back to Scripture. God has worked through gospel movements throughout the centuries since Pentecost. But they do not fit into a mold. Some start from within the church, with revitalization and mobilization. Others are ignited among the unreached by itinerant evangelists. We have outlined things they have in common: Spiritual vitality, discipleship culture, generational multiplication, levels of maturity, pioneering leaders, facilitative catalysts, indigenous forms, and appropriate support systems. They emerge when the gospel penetrates with power through hard-fought spiritual battle. They are spurred on by fervent prayer and faithful obedience to the Great Commission. They flourish where discipleship is the soil in which churches grow.

By looking at gospel movements in the New Testament, missions history, and contemporary case-study, we conclude that gospel movements are relevant and needed throughout the world. However, obstacles stand in the way. Where Christianity has long been part of the landscape, tradition, polity, and extrabiblical expectations stifle movement. Some branches of the church may be revitalized by adopting major changes; but in many cases new beginnings are required. No cosmetic change will generate new waves of gospel expansion. Transformation must come from the inside. Therefore, leaders of established movements face questions like: What really matters? What must we embrace, and what must we release? We must let go of lesser things and we must decide what they are.

LESSER AND GREATER THINGS

CPM adherents who advocate simple churches led by lay people have a hard time finding middle ground with ecclesial conservatives who prioritize theologically trained pastors. Even among CPM practitioners there are different schools of thought when it comes to strategies and tactics. Movement thinkers get caught up in friendly squabbles over *methods and metrics*.

New advances in difficult places require collaboration—unity on essentials, tolerance on secondary things, and charity in everything. Dialogue is helpful but division and independence are not. Are not pet programs, traditions, and methods among the lesser things? Scripture does not prescribe the best methodology. One CPM researcher found that "the data clearly suggest that a particular methodology is far less significant in catalyzing movements than may have been assumed or publicized."[1] His study shows that leader traits and competencies are better movement predictors than the methods used.[2]

Some argue that the *superior results* of CPM practitioners should compel traditional churches to change. Make no mistake—results are important. But are they what really matters? Even the apostles experienced varied

1. Prinz, "Person, Not Method," para. 6.
2. Prinz, "Person, Not Method," para. 6.

results. Some hearers believed, but most rejected the message. When there was a bumper crop, the apostles rejoiced (Acts 6:7; 2 Thess 3:1). But they also rejoiced when they suffered rejection and persecution for his name's sake (Acts 4:41; 16:25). No missiologist can guarantee good results, and even if he or she could, who knows how long they would last? Movements have their ups and downs.

Are we focused on *speedy advance* instead of reproductive patterns and principles? Steve Smith believed we could *hasten the day of Christ's return* through more passionate and concerted effort based on his understanding of 2 Pet 3:12.[3] But an alternative translation to "hasten" his return is *to strive for its coming*. Are we not being short sighted when we focus on speed or numbers? Haste is not a biblical value and can even be counterproductive. There is joy in reaping, but someone must do the hard, slow pioneering work of preparing the soil and sowing. We have seen that gospel movements have a pattern of generational reproduction of disciples and leaders. When this takes place consistently churches reproduce, and movements are born.

WHAT MATTERS MOST

If those are "lesser things," what then should unite those who want to fulfill the Great Commission? God's reputation must shine preeminently. First, he must be glorified by our lives—by who we are, not just by what we accomplish. Much harm is done when cultural and personal preferences take center stage. We compare and compete. We lift ourselves up and diminish our brothers and sisters. Gospel movements must bring glory to God alone. No one else should take credit.

Secondly, God is glorified when we faithfully obey what he has commanded us to do and give him our very best in his strength. We are called to be servants, not critics who pass judgment (1 Cor 4:1–5). We should examine *ourselves* and the *movement in which we serve* before we find fault with others.

1. What is the spiritual temperature of most leaders in the movement? Is prayer frequent and fervent? Is a posture of humble expectation, sacrifice, and devoted service widespread?

2. Are disciples being made, matured, and multiplied? Is witness consistent and are people equipped to share their faith? Could most people articulate what God expects of them as disciples and are they advancing on an identifiable discipleship pathway?

3. Smith, "Our Response," 211.

3. Is the discipleship pathway supported by a reproductive process so that disciples grow and reproduce? Who are the disciple makers and how are they developed?

4. Are indigenous forms and methods being used and local leaders being developed from within the movement? Does leadership development keep pace with numerical growth?

5. Are leaders aware and agreed about the stage of the movement and the spiritual state of its people? Is revitalization needed? Are there stage-appropriate support systems that support healthy growth?

Thirdly, we must work collaboratively with like-minded Christians outside our movement, in a spirit of love and unity. Many of us live in individualistic cultures that put personal rights and preferences before unity. Jesus prayed that we be one, as he is one with his Father (John 17). When we focus on lesser things, we often sacrifice what gives him pleasure, that spirit of oneness, and grieve the Spirit unites us. Is this spirit of collaboration producing joint efforts of prayer, new gospel initiatives, and church-planting networks? If not, we should ask ourselves if unity is only an aspirational value, rather than a real goal.

THE WAY FORWARD

Thus, putting these three priorities together, what matters most is working in unity to make and mature disciples who reproduce in faithful obedience to the Great Commission so that God is glorified. Will we work together to make every disciple a disciple-maker? What we do matters. Jesus left us a command to obey and a pattern to follow.

The task may seem daunting and the current state of things disheartening. But God is not looking for experts, he is looking for courageous obedience. It helps to remember how God used the *first generation of disciples*. It is also true that we may well be the *last generation of disciples*. We live between those two generations and should keep both squarely in sight.

A First-Generation Perspective

We need a fresh look at what God did through *the first generation*. That handful of disparate and uneducated disciples, who fled for their lives at Gethsemane, became an unstoppable force. What resources did Jesus leave with them? He gave his promise to be with them, his Spirit to enable them, and his teaching to guide them—no salaries, no schools, no buildings, no bank accounts. He did not even distribute an instruction manual. He loved them, taught them, and modeled what he taught. Then he commanded them to go and make disciples. They went and gospel spread to the entire Roman world in four decades, one church starting another and one gospel movement giving birth to another.

Most first-generation churches were launched by local disciples who shared the message far and wide. They passed on the message and discipled those who believed. Without the human and material resources we have today, these ordinary men and women impacted the world (Acts 4:13). They invited the Spirit to fill them, guide them, and open doors to the gospel. And they obeyed Christ without compromise. Their story should inspire us to follow in their footsteps. We have the same resources at our disposal, and so much more. The examples in this book give testimony to what can happen when his people prioritize disciple making and faithfully raise up disciple makers.

Finally, we must step forward and invite others to join us in recommitting ourselves to the unfinished task. Garrison aptly said, "There are no passengers in church planting movements,"[4] nor should there be any in his church. If we affirm the priesthood and gifting of all believers, we will disciple and equip every Christian to be part of Christ's labor force. This requires a return to the pattern found in Eph 4:11–12: The theologically trained equip the saints for the work of the ministry instead of doing all the ministry themselves.

A Final-Generation Perspective

We also need the perspective of *the final generation*, the sense of responsibility that comes from reflecting on the end, on Christ's return. We must keep our eyes on this finish line. Jesus has promised that all peoples will receive the gospel, and then the end will come (Matt 24:14). Whether we are that final generation or not, we can be assured that the Great Commission can and will be completed.

> The completion of this mission to all people is not in question. The vision of Revelation is the coming reality. God will bring it to pass. His mission will not be adapted, compromised, or aborted along the way . . . Human frailty will not hinder it, and Satan will not derail it. The Holy Spirit will empower it and divine decree has assured it. The only question is, Will we be taken

4. Garrison, "Something Is Happening," 86.

up in its fulfillment, or will we remain on the sidelines watching as God works through others?[5]

It will take more than an occasional rally to finish the task—although those are needed. There is still difficult work ahead. Completing the mission remains a formidable challenge requiring consistent effort and costly battle. Researchers at the *Joshua Project* tell us that there are about five thousand people groups with no evidence of a viable gospel movement. They represent a quarter of the world's population. One-fourth of the world lives among frontier people groups (FPGs) with little chance of hearing about Jesus. FPGs are a subset of unreached people groups that have 0.1% or fewer who identify with Jesus in any way. The thirty-one largest FPGs add up to almost one billion people.[6]

Furthermore, a closer look at the major FPGs reveals that they are in resistant places, largely in Hindu and Muslim-majority contexts. Many unreached people groups are hard to access because of geographic and logistical barriers, such as nomadic tribes and Himalayan peoples. Political restrictions stand in the way in Bhutan and North Korea. The situation is exacerbated when governments implement anti-conversion laws establishing one religion at the expense of others. Trying to reach a Hindu or Muslim with the gospel may lead to imprisonment or death by a frenzied mob.

The threat from extremists is even worse. At a conference in Thailand, we received word that an outspoken Indonesian evangelist was abducted at gun point. One lady broke out crying uncontrollably, knowing it meant certain death. A group of Islamic extremists had earlier threatened the evangelist's life and the government had warned him to keep quiet. He had not complied, and the authorities turned a blind eye as religious extremists carried out their threat. His wife said that he had counted the cost and was prepared for the ultimate sacrifice. That did not lessen the family's pain. They mourned as they continued their missionary work without him.

We work toward multiplication, knowing that it will take maturity to sustain it. We hope for rapid growth and persevere when it is beyond our horizon. The victories of the first generation of Christians, despite scant resources, should inspire us. Christ's assurance that the task will be completed should strengthen our resolve. The Baum family, whose story follows, embraced this twin perspective of *first and final generations* when they decided to devote their lives to reaching Muslim Turks.[7]

5. Ott, *Church on Mission*, 85.

6. "Pray for the 31," ii.

7. This case study is based on written reports from Paul Baum and interviews with him between 2000 and 2018.

CATALYZING A MOVEMENT
AMONG BULGARIAN TURKS

By some estimates, Turkey is the largest unreached country in the world. Ninety-nine percent of its inhabitants are Muslims. Seventy percent of the Turkish nationals living outside of Turkey reside in Germany, primarily in urban centers like Berlin and the Ruhr Region. The Baum family prayed and sought to reach Turks for many years. They served three years in Wiesbaden, Germany, and then lived in Turkey from 1990 to 1991, to learn Turkish language and culture.

When they returned to Germany, they settled in the Ruhr region, which had the largest concentration of Turks. By this time, their teammates had left Germany for various reasons. During the years that followed, they established relationships with both German and Turkish believers. They struggled with the lack of fruit and the isolation, being the only workers in the entire region with a million Turks. The burden felt overwhelming at times. However, in 1993, five Turkish-speakers came to the Lord, and then one or two each year after that.

Then in 2000, a German medical student asked Paul Baum for evangelistic literature to share with a Turkish acquaintance. Paul suggested to the student that they pray together monthly for his friend and other Turks in the region—about 14 percent of the population. They invited others to join them, and the monthly prayer meeting grew.

In September 2001, they were asked by a pastor if they had any interest in establishing a ministry center in the neighboring town of Duisburg and they started looking at buildings that could serve that purpose. With God's help, what Paul had previously considered impossible became a reality. Within five months, *Die Brücke* (The Bridge) ministry center began outreach to Turkish immigrants as a nonprofit organization.

About 70 percent of their neighborhood was Turkish. Sensing God's leading, the Baum family moved there in 2002. Die Brücke became a meeting place where Germans and Turks could come together, and where German believers could show them God's love in practical ways. For the German believers, who often find Turkish culture strange or frightening, they offered *Discovery Day* seminars with neighborhood walks to meet Turkish neighbors. They befriended and helped Turks who wanted German citizenship by walking with them through the immigration process. Paul explains:

> When we first arrived, we immediately began to help with language lessons, reading lessons, and I did translation for them

to register, go to the doctor, to the school, etc. They recognized our help and love for them. Some have said that we were sent by God to help them. We have also been doing children's weeks, homework help, etc. They are poor, and fall through the social services cracks, so we have become advocates for them in official government contexts.[8]

But their vision went beyond helping Turks integrate into life in Germany. The Baum family and their German partners developed three goals: (1) Planting house churches through personal evangelism, small group Bible studies, and compassion ministry; (2) Supporting Turkish churches and believers through spiritual input (modeling, teaching, and discipling) and resources (literature and meeting places); (3) Training believers to do outreach among Turkish people to multiply the workers.

Short-term teams came to Duisburg to work with Turkish youth using the center. Favorable contacts were made with several families. From 2005 to 2008, Turkish believers from all over Europe came together quarterly at Die Brücke, totaling about two hundred MBBs. They came from churches in Switzerland, France, the Netherlands, Belgium, and Germany. Turkish neighbors watched this happen, and an imam came to speak with Paul, asking for a Bible at the end of the conversation.

The first Bulgarian Turks arrived in Duisburg in December 2007. In July 2009, God opened a special door for the Turks to emigrate from Bulgaria, as Bulgaria became a part of the European Union. Many of them heard about the help provided by *Die Brücke* and went there rather than to the local mosque. Christians helped them settle in their new land.

Within four months, they began a weekly Bible study which grew to about twenty-five Bulgarian Turks. Many of these former Muslims came to the Lord. Two eight-year-old girls who came for homework help said that they had dreams about the Baum family before meeting them. One family was freed of demonic influences and others were healed. The new believers invited others, and, for a while, people were coming to Christ weekly—primarily through relationships and outreaches of the ministry center. Two Bible study groups began.

Later that year, both groups began meeting as local assemblies for worship, one in Turkish and the other in Bulgarian, each having their own leaders. In 2009, about seventy MBBs met on Monday evenings and up to forty-five Bulgarian Turks also gathered for a Saturday evening worship service. Disciples offered prayer for Turkish neighbors, and several older Turkish Muslims approached Paul for prayers on their behalf. The local

8. Baum, "Die Brücke," 5.

Turkish mosque, at that time the largest in Germany, even displayed books for children about Jesus' love provided by *Die Brücke*.

Some Bulgarian Turks secretly took video clips of the local meetings and sent them through the Internet to family and friends back home in Bulgaria. These clips stimulated a response from Bulgaria. The pastor of one of the Turkish churches in Duisburg was invited to visit Bulgaria in 2013. He took *Jesus Film* videos and testimonial DVDs with him. The Baum family has heard reports of over four hundred Turks coming to the Lord in Bulgaria. According to Baum, this ingathering fed a 1989 revival that started when after a boy from a Muslim family was healed after prayer in Jesus' name. His father, a well-known man in the community, turned to Christ and started sharing his faith in him. As a result, between two and five thousand came to faith in Christ.

Tragically, a conflict led to a split into two groups, and eventually to separate Bulgarian-speaking and Turkish-speaking congregations. Paul and a Turkish woman helped them reconcile just before Baum family returned to the United States for a year of home assignment. Both congregations grew and each started daughter churches while they were away. Then the Bulgarian fellowship started another church which, in turn, gave birth to a granddaughter church.

In 2002, the Baum family started their ministry with two Turkish-speaking families. By 2018, there were four generations of Turkish congregations totaling twenty churches. Paul estimated that, at that time, there were about eleven churches with a weekly involvement of six hundred to seven hundred within thirty minutes of *Die Brücke*.

The churches vary in size between thirty-five and three hundred. They are reproducing as Christians move to other towns or share the gospel with relatives in other places. In one case, a new group used a speaker connected through the telephone line to join a worship service taking place in another city.

Multiplication is taking place among Muslim-background Turks. The Baum family could have left at several junctures, but they stayed. They prayed that the gospel would breakthrough, and it did! Together with another organization, they are developing a Bible school and have found some good potential teachers.

Conclusion

Today, hundreds of humble gospel movement facilitators like Paul and Kathy Baum contribute what they can to a future that is not their own. But more are needed. In many ways, the start of this millennium resembles the situation described in the book of Acts, chapters 8–12. God was on the move, and lay witnesses were crossing frontiers with the gospel. They lacked training but were brimming with spiritual zeal. Meanwhile, the apostles, experienced and commissioned to lead the missionary charge, were hunkered down in Jerusalem. Today, many who have theological education, rich ministry experience, and cross-cultural sensitivities are disconnected from God's global work through gospel movements.

There has been great progress toward the goal of emerging gospel movements in most people groups, but much arduous work remains. The sacrifice of planters and missionaries in these spiritually arid and hostile lands reminds us that we will not prevail by might or strength but by his Spirit. Theirs is often thankless and risky work. When catalysts come alongside these brave servants, it is not only a privilege but also an awesome responsibility.

The approach used in one place will not necessarily serve God's purposes in another. Completing the task will take diverse and culturally appropriate gospel initiatives that pull together local leaders and external catalysts, like the ones we describe in these chapters. The results may not look like CPMs initially, and some may never rise to that stature, but they will transform lives, neighborhoods, and cities over time.

These gospel movement initiatives will require humble cooperation and multicultural partnerships. All are called to serve, not to possess or control ministries. Those who are well resourced should help the less favored, and together discover and deploy ministries that are fruitful and sustainable. Only Spirit-led cooperation will lead to God-glorifying gospel movements among every people group.

We have not arrived. Most of the Christian labor force is deployed where the church already exists, rather than where it is most needed. Only 3 percent serve among the least reached. We continually strive to observe, learn, listen, and evaluate, because God is always doing new things. This book should be a wake-up call for us, a plea to join the action, and a guide to do so strategically. If you would like to access practical resources to grow as a catalyst, please visit the website: www.churchplantingcatalyst.com.

Appendix

Three Types of Church-Planting Movements: DMM, T4T, and PMC[1]

VISION AND MOTIVATION

All three types of movement initially involve cross-cultural messengers who desire to see disciples and churches multiply, believing that God brings the increase, and prayer waters the gospel seed. They emphasize disciple-making through obedience-based, Word-centered discipleship groups which lead to the formation of leaders and churches. In all, equipping to make new disciples is done primarily "on the job."

STARTING POINT AND DISCIPLING METHOD

Although these CPMs end up with similar distinguishing marks documented by Garrison (2004), they evolve differently. *T4T* disciples those who are already Christians and equips them to make disciples through their relational networks, while in PMC and DMM local Christians are trained to find bridge people or people of peace in society.

In *T4T* the gospel is usually shared in one presentation and people are invited to trust Christ. New believers go through a series of five lessons to establish them in the faith. Within six weeks someone can receive the basics, share them with others, and become part of a house church. In DMM,

1. Smith and Parks, "T4T or DMM."

147

discipleship is *to Christ,* beginning with pre-Christian people of peace. These seekers discover Bible truth over an extended period using Discovery Bible Studies and Bible narratives that unpack the redemption story woven through Scripture.

BREAKOUT POINT

People movements to Christ take off when a critical mass, often a significant minority group, turns to Christ. DMMs reach the breakout point when disciple-making streams that use DBS start to multiply, resulting in new churches. In *T4T* simple churches reproduce over several generations, because the disciple-making groups that give birth to them multiply and start new streams.

This comparison underlines the fact that God uses different pathways and disciple-making approaches to give birth to gospel movements. Even those who espouse CPM values differ in their methodology to reach generational reproduction. Recent studies indicate that movements combine multiple methods and that the profile of the movement leaders is more significant than the means employed.

Bibliography

Addison, Steve. *Movements That Change the World: Five Keys to Spreading the Gospel.* Downers Grove: InterVarsity, 2011.

———. *Pioneering Movements: Leadership That Multiplies Disciples and Churches.* Downers Grove: InterVarsity, 2015.

———. *The Rise and Fall of Movements: A Roadmap for Leaders.* N.p.: 100Movements, 2019. Kindle edition.

———. *What Jesus Started: Joining the Movement Changing the World.* Downers Grove: InterVarsity, 2012.

Allen, Roland. *The Spontaneous Expansion of the Church and the Causes Which Hinder It.* 1927. Reprint, Grand Rapids: Eerdmans, 1962.

Amelia, Rosa. "Iglesia Los Pinos Nuevos (Falcón)." *EcuRed.* https://www.ecured.cu/Iglesia_Los_Pinos_Nuevos_(Falcón)#Inicio_de_la_Obra.

Austvold, Steve. "Superintendent's Ministry Report." May 2017.

Baum, Paul. "Die Brücke Ministry Report." June 2019.

Behar, Lee. "Reflection on a Missions Partnership." *MissionNexus,* April 1, 2008. https://missionexus.org/reflection-on-a-missions-partnership.

Bonhoeffer, Dietrich. *The Cost of Discipleship.* 1937. Reprint, New York: Touchstone, 1995.

Bruce, F. F. *The Book of Acts.* Grand Rapids: Eerdmans, 1977.

———. *New Testament History.* Garden City: Doubleday, 1969.

Burns, James. *Revival: It's Laws and Leaders.* London: Hodder and Stoughton, 1909.

Christopherson, Jeff. "So What Comes After Church Growth?" *SEND Network,* September 6, 2018. https://www.namb.net/send-network/resource/so-what-comes-after-church-growth.

Coles, David, and Stan Parks, eds. *24:14—A Testimony to All Peoples.* Spring, TX: 24:14, 2019.

Corbett, Steve, and Brian Fikkert. *When Helping Hurts: Effective Poverty Alleviation.* Chicago: Moody, 2009.

Das, Kiran Kumar. "The Growth of Christianity in Nepal." *Bible Living Ministries Nepal.* http://www.biblelivingministries.org/nepal_missions.

Davis, Ray. "Missions History: On the Cusp of a New Era of Modern Missions." *IMB,* September 7, 2017. https://www.imb.org/2017/0/07/have-we-entered-a-new-era-of-modern-missions.

Davis, Titus. "Evangelical Free Church of West Africa Report." Summer 2010.

Esler, Ted. "Coming to Terms: Two Church Planting Paradigms." *IJFM* 30 (2013) 67–73.

Fraser, J. O. *Fraser and Prayer*. London: Missionary Fellowship, 1963.

Garrison, David. *Church Planting Movements: How God Is Redeeming a Lost World*. Midlothian, TX: WIGTake, 2004.

———. "Global Church Planting: Something Is Happening." *Journal of Evangelism and Missions 4* (2005), 77-87.

Green, Michael. *Evangelism in the Early Church*. Grand Rapids: Eerdmans, 1970.

Gupta, Paul R., and Sherwood G. Lingenfelter. *Breaking Tradition to Accomplish Vision: Training Leaders for Church-Planting Movements*. Winona Lake, IN: BMH, 2006.

Hiebert, Paul. *Anthropological Insights for Missionaries*. Grand Rapids: Baker, 1985.

———. *The Gospel in Human Contexts: Anthropological Explorations for Contemporary Missions*. Grand Rapids: Baker Academic, 2009.

Hunt, David F. "A Revolution in Church Multiplication in East Africa: Transformational Leaders Develop a Self-Sustainable Model of Rapid Church Multiplication." DMin diss., Bakke Graduate University, Seattle, 2009.

Johnson, Todd M. *Christianity in Its Global Context, 1970–2020. Society, Religion, and Mission*. South Hamilton, MA: Center for the Study of Global Christianity, Gordon-Conwell Theological Seminary, 2013.

Johnstone, Patrick, and Jason Mandryk. *Operation World*. 6th ed. Waynesboro, GA: Paternoster, 2001.

Julien, Thomas. "ACT Strategy: Apostolic Church-Planting Team Strategy (2.0)." Strategy paper. Grace Brethren International Missions, 2000.

Keller, Timothy. *Center Church: Doing Balanced, Gospel-Centered Ministry in Your City*. Grand Rapids: Zondervan, 2012.

———. "Defining a Gospel Movement." *City to City* (a Medium.com site), May 9, 2018. https://medium.com/redeemer-city-to-city/defining-a-gospel-movement-c4f591e919b9.

Kwon, Lilian. "Top 25 Multiplying Churches in America." *Christian Post*, June 26, 2007. https://www.christianpost.com/news/top-25-multiplying-churches-in-america.html.

LaTourette, Kenneth Scott. *The First Five Centuries*. New York: Harper, 1937.

Long, Justin. "One Percent of the World: A Macroanalysis of 1,369 Movements to Christ." *Mission Frontiers* 42 (2020) 37-42.

MacDonald, Jeffrey. "Rise of Sunshine Samaritans: On a Mission or Holiday?" *Christian Science Monitor*, May 25, 2006. https://www.csmonitor.com/2006/0525/p01s01-ussc.html.

Mandryk, Jason. *Operation World: The Definitive Prayer Guide to Every Nation*. Colorado Springs: Biblica, 2010.

McConnell, Walter. "God's Mission to the Lisu." *OMF Journal for Reflective Practitioners* 14 (Jan-Apr 2019) 24-34.

McGavran, Donald. *Understanding Church Growth*. Grand Rapids: Eerdmans, 1970.

Meeks, Wayne. *The First Urban Christians: The Social World of the Apostle Paul*. New Haven: Yale University Press, 2003.

Miller, Matthew. "The Role of Outsider Leaders in Disciple Making Movements in East Africa." DMin diss., Bakke Graduate University, Seattle, 2015.

Morgan, Timothy. "A Fresh Encounter with Jesus." *Christianity Today*, July 25, 2013. https://www.christianitytoday.com/ct/2013/july-august/fresh-encounter-with-jesus.html.

Moses, B. D. B. "The Baptists of Nagaland." *Moses on Missions*, April 30, 2008. http://mosesonmissions.wordpress.com/2008/04/30/the-baptists-of-nagaland.

———. "Edwin Clark—Missionary to Naga of India." *Moses on Missions*, November 29, 2008. https://mosesonmissions.wordpress.com/2008/11/29/edwin-clark-missionary-to-naga-of-india/.

Muriu, Oscar. "The African Planter: An Interview with Oscar Muriu." *Leadership Journal*, April 1, 2007. https://www.christianitytoday.com/le/2007/002/3.96.html.

Orr, J. Edwin. *Evangelical Awakenings in India in the Early Twentieth Century*. New Delhi: Masihi Sahitya Sanstha, 1970.

———. *The Second Evangelical Awakening: An Account of the Second Worldwide Evangelical Revival Beginning in the Mid-Nineteenth Century*. Fort Washington, PA: CLC, 1964.

Ott, Craig. *The Church on Mission: A Biblical Vision for Transformation among All People*. Grand Rapids: Baker Academic, 2019.

———. "Movement Maturity and Missionary Participation." *EMQ* 54 (Winter 2017) 8–12.

Ott, Craig, and Gene Wilson. *Global Church Planting: Biblical Principles and Best Practices for Multiplication*. Grand Rapids: Baker Academic, 2011.

Peters, George. *Saturation Evangelism*. Grand Rapids: Zondervan, 1970.

Pickett, J. Waskom. *Christian Mass Movements in India*. New York: Abingdon, 1933.

Pierard, R. "John Livingston Nevius (1829–1893)." In *The New International Dictionary of the Christian Church*, edited by J. D. Douglas, 700. Grand Rapids: Zondervan, 1974.

Pinney, Jay. "Catalyzing Church Planting Movements." *Catalyzer Training Manual*, 2018.

———. "Eternal Perspectives." Ministry Report. April 5, 2019.

"Pray for the 31—Prayer Guide: An Invitation to the Global Body of Christ." *Joshua Project*, 2019. https://joshuaproject.net/assets/media/handouts/the31.pdf.

Preston, Frank. "A Study on Scripture Engagement in DMMs." *EMQ* 56 (April–June 2020). https://missionexus.org/a-study-on-scripture-engagement-in-dmms/.

Prinz, Emanuel. "The Person, Not the Method: An Essential Ingredient for Catalyzing a Movement." With Dave Coles. *Mission Frontiers Online*, July–August 2021. https://www.missionfrontiers.org/issue/article/the-person-not-the-method-an-essential-ingredient-for-catalyzing-a-movement.

Ramsay, William. *Saint Paul the Traveler and the Roman Citizen*. Grand Rapids: Baker, 1982.

Reynolds, Jeffrey Paul. "Dawson Trotman's Personal Spiritual Disciplines as the Foundation for His Great Commission Ministry." PhD diss., Southern Baptist Theological Seminary, Louisville, Kentucky, 2014.

Richardson, Don. *Eternity in Their Hearts*. Ventura, CA: Regal, 1986.

Robb, John. "Prayer as a Strategic Weapon in Frontier Missions." *ISFM*, September 13–15, 1990.

Rodriguez, Omar. "Latin America Ministry Report." April 2015.

———. "Latin America Ministry Report." April 2018.

Sanders, J. Oswald. *Spiritual Leadership*. Chicago: Moody, 1980.

Schindler, Dietrich. "Church Planting Multiplication from a European Perspective." Paper presented at Exponential Conference, Orlando, 2010.

Selenga, Nubako. "ReachAfrica Ministry Report." March–May 2012.

Shank, Nathan. "Multiplying Movement Pioneers." Interview with Steve Smith. *Movements* (blog), June 13, 2017. https://www.movements.net/blog/blog/2017/6/12/141-multiplying-movement-pioneers-nathan-shank.

Shank, Nathan, and Kari Shank. "Four Fields of Kingdom Growth: Starting and Releasing Healthy Churches," 2015. https://www.movements.net/blog/2015/06/01/nathan-shank-on-the-four-fields-podcast.html?rq=shank.

Smith, Steve. "A Profile of a Movement Catalyst." *Mission Frontiers* (2014) 38–41.

———. "Finishing the Task." Interviewed with Steve Addison. May 21, 2018. https://vimeo.com/271207196.

Smith, Steve, and Ying Kai. *T4T: A Discipleship Re-revolution; The Story behind the World's Fastest Growing Church Planting Movement and How It Can Happen in Your Community.* Midlothian: WIGTake, 2011.

Smith, Steve, and Stan Parks. "T4T or DMM (DBS): Only God Can Start a Church-Planting Movement." *Mission Frontiers,* January–February 2015. http://www.missionfrontiers.org/issue/article/t4t-or-dmm-dbs-only-god-can-start-a-church-planting-movement-part-1-of-2.

Stark, Rodney. *The Rise in Christianity: How the Obscure, Marginal Jesus Movement Became the Dominant Religious Force in the Western World in a Few Centuries.* San Francisco: HarperSanFrancisco, 1997.

Steele, Francis. *Not in Vain: The Story of the North Africa Mission.* Pasadena: William Carey, 1981.

Steffen, Tom. *The Facilitator Era: Beyond Pioneer Church Multiplication.* Eugene, OR: Wipf & Stock, 2011.

Stetzer, Ed, and David Garrison. "The Potential for Church Planting Movements in the Western World." http://www.murraymoerman.com/3downloads/cp/cpm_in_western_world-stetzer,garrison.pdf.

Trousdale, Jerry, and Glenn Sunshine. *The Kingdom Unleashed: How Jesus's 1st-Century Kingdom Values Are Transforming Thousands of Cultures and Awakening His Church.* Murfreesboro, TN: DMM Library, 2018.

Untener, Kenneth. "A Prayer of Oscar Romero." *Bread for the World*, October 26, 2018. https://www.bread.org/blog/prayer-oscar-romero.

Urbanek, Kurt. *Cuba's Great Awakening: Church Planting Movement in Cuba.* Fort Worth, TX: Church Starting Network, 2015.

Ward, Reginald. *The Protestant Evangelical Awakening.* Cambridge: Cambridge University Press, 1992.

Warneck, Gustav. *History of Protestant Missions.* Edinburgh: Oliphant, 1906.

Watson, David, and Paul D. Watson. *Contagious Disciple Making: Leading Others on a Journey of Discovery.* Nashville: Nelson, 2014.

Weber, Hans-Ruedi. *The Layman in Christian History: A Project of the Department on the Laity of the World Council of Churches.* London: SCM, 2000.

Weyandt, Craig. "Multiplying Transformational Churches among All People." Ministry newsletter, December 2019.

Wilson, Gene. "Church-Planting Catalysts for Gospel Movements" *EMQ* 52 (2016) 272–81.

———. "Holistic Church Planting: Moving beyond Polemics to Obedience." *EMQ* 50 (2014) 342–49.

Winter, Ralph, and Steve Hawthorne. "Four Men, Three Eras, Two Transitions." In *Perspectives on the World Christian Movement*, edited by Ralph Winter, B33–43. Pasadena, CA: William Carey, 1992.

Wittwer, Joseph. "Planting More Churches." Life Center Church website, February 24, 2013. https://lifecenter.net/sermons/2013/planting-more-churches.

Zurlo, Gina, et al. "World Christianity and Mission 2020: Ongoing Shift to the Global South." *IBMR* 44 (2020) 8–19.

Made in the USA
Monee, IL
19 January 2023

25635757R00098